country garden planner

Written by Darrell Trout

Country Home® Books
Des Moines, Iowa

COUNTRY HOME® BOOKS
AN IMPRINT OF MEREDITH® BOOKS

Country Garden Planner

Executive Garden Editor: Cathy Wilkinson Barash
Writer: Darrell Trout
Art Director: Richard Michels
Copy Chief: Catherine Hamrick
Copy and Production Editor: Terri Fredrickson
Contributing Copy Editor: Karen Weir-Jimerson
Contributing Proofreader: James A. Baggett
Contributing Photographers: Thomas Arledge, Liz Ball, Laurie Black, Ernest Braun,
   David Cavagnaro, Stephen Cridland, Linda & Alan Detrick, Charles Marden Fitch,
   D. Randolph Foulds, Susan Gilmore, Meredith Hebden, Saxon Holt,
   Jon Jensen, Michael Jensen, Dency Kane, Peter Krumhardt, Barbara Martin,
   Julie Maris Semel, Mary Carolyn Pindar, Rick Ray, Eric Roth, William Stites,
   Marilyn Stouffer, Saba S. Tian
Illustrator/Plans: Melanie Marder Parks
Indexer: Donald Glassman
Interns: Laura Davenport, Emily Wilkinson
Electronic Production Coordinator: Paula Forest
Editorial and Design Assistants: Kaye Chabot, Treesa Landry, Karen Schirm
Production Director: Douglas M. Johnston
Production Manager: Pam Kvitne
Assistant Prepress Manager: Marjorie J. Schenkelberg

MEREDITH® BOOKS

Editor in Chief: James D. Blume
Design Director: Matt Strelecki
Managing Editor: Gregory H. Kayko

Director, Sales & Marketing, Retail: Michael A. Peterson
Director, Sales & Marketing, Special Markets: Rita McMullen
Director, Sales & Marketing, Home & Garden Center Channel: Ray Wolf
Director, Operations: George A. Susral

Vice President, General Manager: Jamie L. Martin

COUNTRY HOME® MAGAZINE

Editor in Chief: Carol Sama Sheehan

MEREDITH PUBLISHING GROUP

President, Publishing Group: Christopher M. Little
Vice President, Consumer Marketing & Development: Hal Oringer

MEREDITH CORPORATION

Chairman and Chief Executive Officer: William T. Kerr

Chairman of the Executive Committee: E. T. Meredith III

All of us at Country Home®
Books are dedicated to providing
you with information and ideas
to enhance your home and garden.
We welcome your comments and
suggestions. Write to us at: Country
Home® Books, Garden Editorial
Department, 1716 Locust St., LN-
116, Des Moines, IA 50309-3023.

If you would like to purchase
additional copies of any of our
books, check with your local
bookstore.

Copyright© 1998 by Meredith
Corporation, Des Moines, Iowa. All
rights reserved. Printed in the
United States of America.
First Edition. Printing Number and
Year: 5 4 3 2 1   02 01 00 99 98
Library of Congress Catalog Card
Number: 98-66906
ISBN: 0-696-20848-2

Cover Photograph: John Reed
Forsman

few acts are more inspired, indeed creative, than planning and nurturing your own special garden. We put together *Country Garden Planner* so you can design an outdoor retreat ideally suited to your lifestyle and region.

In these pages, the range and diversity of America's gardens come alive. Truly, they are visions realized by gardeners unsurpassed in their innovation, tenacity, and passion for nature. Whether they live in coastal, rural, small-town, suburban, or urban settings,

these individuals find common ground in embracing the country lifestyle and generously sharing their gardening expertise in this book.

Take your time exploring each garden, presented in rich, vivid photographs and a beautifully illustrated design plan. You can re-create one of the plans or use parts of several to make a unique statement.

You'll quickly learn that color, muted or vibrant, flourishes freely in country gardens. Choose from hundreds of flowers—such as calla lilies, delphiniums, foxgloves, daisies, valerian, pinks, black-eyed Susans, purple coneflowers, roses, and campanulas—to paint

how to make a country garden

your garden in distinctive strokes. Continue the spontaneous theme, allowing plants to spill from beds onto pathways. Let fences, trellises, arbors, and pergolas drip with vines and climbers, just as they do in many of these gardens.

To simplify your selection of plants, we have included an encyclopedia after every plan. A photograph of each plant is featured, as well as specific cultural information and growing tips.

Country Garden Planner will serve you well in any region. Even if you don't live in the same area as the featured gardens, the plants represent various hardiness ranges, so you can use most in your own design. What's more, the mail-order sources on page 186 make all the plants readily available.

The final section "Creating Your Country Garden" shows you how to incorporate classic elements of country style—the hardscape of the garden, including fences, arbors, pergolas and paths. We also tell you how to attract butterflies, songbirds, and hummingbirds to splash your garden with more color and movement.

So wherever you live and whatever size your property, you can plant your own patch of country. It's easy, especially with these plans. And, take joy in every moment of the experience, from working the earth to discovering new colors, textures, scents, and sounds revealed by your own country garden.

table of contents

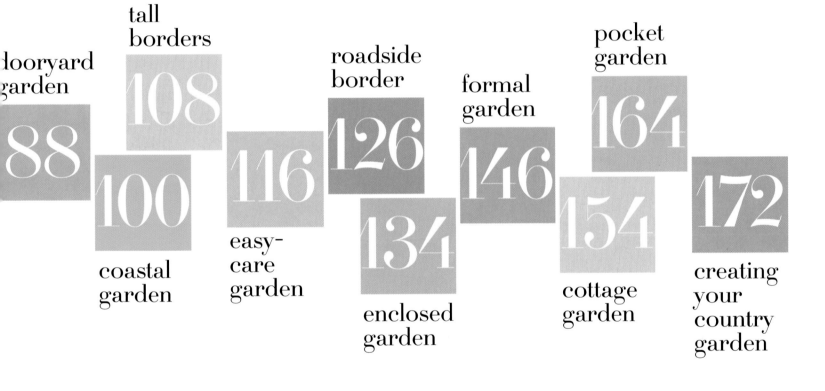

double

border

repeating shapes, textures, colors,

and plants define double borders.

As you walk down the stepping

stone path separating these borders, you appreciate

the aesthetics and strength of an informal design.

Unlike formal English double borders, which are

mirror image, these don't have precise straight

edges. Instead, they have a more informal look, which

was achieved by creating borders of about the

same size and shape and incorporating favorite plants.

Roses and delphiniums are a classic country combination. Opposite: 'Nora Barlow' columbine.

an informal double border

traditional English double borders conjure up visions of formal beauty. In such borders, which often are done on a grand scale, the garden on each side of the path is a mirror image. They're of a size that most of us can't replicate in our own backyards. On old English estates, it is still common to see two borders, each 300 feet long and 20 feet deep, where a crew of trained gardeners keep it looking perfect.

Ed and Carol King's Eugene, Oregon, garden is a far cry from English tradition. Their deep, informal borders aren't married to such demanding maintenance. Like English double border gardens, the Kings'

borders are planned for continuous bloom, but contain many durable, no-fuss plants.

Typically, low-growing plants, such as dianthus, creeping speedwell, wild sweet William, forget-me-nots, and chamomile, are planted near the edge of the border. Like the Kings, you can gain a different perspective by incorporating perennials whose tall, airy flowers rise above the low-growing leaves to create a romantic veil through which you view the garden. *Verbena bonariensis* is one of the best plants for this purpose, with its purple flowers borne on wiry 2- to 3-foot stems. A self-sower, it will grace your garden with its presence year after year.

In a border, the contrasts in foliage texture and color

contribute as much interest as the flowers. Include soft leaves of creeping thyme and lamb's ears, textured leaves of astilbe and heather, and the succulent foliage of 'Autumn Joy' sedum and euphorbia.

Vertical elements add drama and punctuate borders. In this garden, a saucer magnolia, rambling roses, and delphiniums all make bold statements.

Emphasize plants that don't require a lot of

maintenance. Time spent in the garden should be fun—smelling the roses and cutting flowers for bouquets, rather than worrying over fussy plants. Here, the Kings mixed yarrow and speedwell with shrub roses in a carpet of chamomile. And, dianthus, daylilies, and rose campion thrive in the heat of summer.

Follow Carol King's advice: "Never fear trying something new, because if a plant or color combination doesn't work, it gets moved." And, you'll have a garden with lush plantings and plenty of flowers for cutting.

MULTISEASON INTEREST
Most borders are barren in winter, but not if you include some ornamental grasses. The silvery plumes of *Miscanthus* 'Morning Light' and 'Silver Feather' are exquisite in the fall and winter garden. The only time they're not attractive is in early spring after they've been cut down.

Annuals are especially useful to add color early in the year and fill in later in the season. Go beyond the overused petunias, impatiens, and begonias and explore many new introductions in the world of annuals. Look for labeled award-winning plants, such as the All-America Selections, Proven Winners, and Fleuro-select plants, at garden centers and in catalogs.

Swordlike iris leaves contrast well with globular hydrangea flowers. *Opposite*: Overview of the garden.

Local basalt stepping stones define the path

that runs through the double border at Ed and Carol King's home in Eugene, Oregon. The house has a 70-foot long porch overlooking portions of the borders. From the porch, you can walk down to the path which leads you through the dramatic borders and quiet sitting areas. The path is wide enough to allow two people to stroll comfortably and admire the garden, yet it feels cozy and intimate. The borders are structured, but have a country, informal feeling because of the billowing, lush plants used in them. The stepping-stone path adds to the informality.

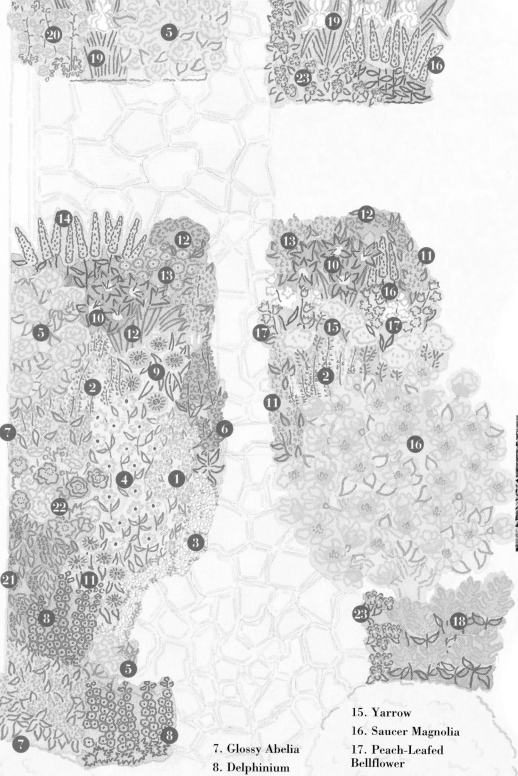

heather

Calluna vulgaris
'Lyndon Proudley'
• Shrub, evergreen
• 6", spread to 12"
• Late summer-fall
• Lavender
• Zones 5-7
• Sun, partial shade
• Source: w
Evergreen groundcover
that blooms late in the
summer. Easy if planted
in acid, well-drained,
sandy soil.

wild sweet william

Phlox divaricata
• Perennial
• 12"
• Spring
• Blue
• Zones 4-9
• Part shade, shade
• Sources: gg, jj

Semievergreen
groundcover; spreads.
Good interplanted with
late spring bulbs.
Performs well under
trees. Prefers moist,
organic soil. Cut back
after it finishes
flowering.

chamomile

Chamaemelum nobile
• Perennial, herb
• 9-12"
• Late spring-late
summer
• Fragrant
• White
• Zones 3-10
• Sun, part shade
• Sources: j, s, t, v
An old-fashioned, apple-
scented groundcover;
cannot bear heavy foot
traffic. Mow for a
chamomile "lawn."
Easy to grow in well-
drained soil. Dry for
teas and tisanes.

1. Wild Sweet William
2. Heather
3. Chamomile
4. Black-Eyed Susan
5. Floribunda Rose
6. Cardinal Flower
7. Glossy Abelia
8. Delphinium
9. Blanket Flower
10. Daylily
11. Creeping Speedwell
12. Pinks
13. Rose Campion
14. Speedwell
15. Yarrow
16. Saucer Magnolia
17. Peach-Leafed Bellflower
18. Astilbe
19. Bearded Iris
20. Columbine
21. Heavenly Bamboo
22. Shirley Poppy
23. Pansy

black-eyed susan

Rudbeckia hyb.
- Perennial or annual
- 2-7'
- Summer, fall
- Yellow with black
- Zones 3-9
- Sun
- Sources: s, gg

Masses of flowers all summer. Good in borders or wild areas.

floribunda rose

Rosa 'Apricot Nectar'
- Shrub
- 4-5'
- Summer
- Fragrant
- Apricot-pink
- Zones 5-10
- Sun
- Sources: v, gg

All-American Rose Selection. Beautiful, 4-inch, double flowers; several to a cluster. Delightfully fruity fragrance. Reliable repeat bloom. Glossy leaves and bushy growth habit.

cardinal flower

Lobelia x *speciosa* 'Border Scarlet'
- Perennial
- 18-60"
- Summer
- Scarlet

- Zones 3-9
- Sun, part shade
- Source: u

Vigorous, tough plants. Attractive dark stems. Plant where it receives the glow of early morning or late afternoon sun. Divide plants in spring every 2 or 3 years.

glossy abelia

Abelia x *grandiflora*
- Shrub
- 3-6'
- Late spring to frost
- White, pink flush
- Zones 6-9
- Sun, part shade
- Sources: n, ff

Delicate flowers with long season of bloom. Excellent in mass plantings or on banks to prevent erosion. Easy to grow in moist, acid soil. Prune out deadwood when necessary.

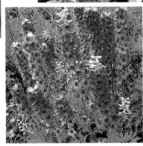

delphinium

Delphinium elatum hyb.
- Perennial
- 3-8'
- Spring, summer
- Blue to white
- Zones 3-10
- Sun, light shade
- Sources: s, cc, ii

Elegant, stately plants, which unfortunately are short-lived. Dislike heat. Add new plants each year for best effect. Excellent cut flowers.

blanket flower

Gaillardia pulchella
- Annual
- 12-24"
- Late spring, summer
- Red, yellows
- All zones
- Sun

- Source: r

Showy 2- to 3-inch flowers. Many cultivars with single and bicolors; also double-flowered varieties. Sow seed indoors; transplant outside after danger of frost is past.

daylily

Hemerocallis 'Chicago Regal'
- Perennial
- 30"
- Spring
- Purple with pink
- Zones 3-10
- Sun, part shade
- Source: w

Durable and long-blooming 6-inch flowers. Prefers deep, rich, well-drained soil. Divide every 3 to 5 years. Interplant with daffodils.

creeping speedwell

Veronica prostrata 'Rosea'
- Perennial
- 6-10"
- Late spring, summer
- Purple-pink to blue
- Zones 5-8
- Sun, part shade
- Source: bb

Free-flowering, creeping plant. Needs well-drained soil. Does not like rich soil; grow in poor or lean soil. Easy to propagate by layering stems.

pinks

Dianthus 'Zing Rose'
- Perennial
- 6"
- Summer
- Fragrant
- Rose
- Zones 3-8
- Sun
- Sources: b, s, ii

Grasslike leaves. Needs well-drained soil; add lime for best fragrance.

rose campion

Lychnis coronaria
- Perennial
- 18-36"
- Summer
- Magenta
- Zones 3-10
- Sun
- Sources: e, j, z

Spreading, silvery-woolly leaves are a foil for bright flowers. Grows best in poor, well-drained soil. Short-lived, but will self-sow.

speedwell

Veronica Spicata 'Blue Charm'
- Perennial
- 24"
- Early summer
- Lavender-blue
- Zones 3-10
- Sun, part shade

- Sources: e, b, j, ii

Compact plant with many 3-inch flower spikes. Cut back flowering stems for repeat bloom. Attracts butterflies. Easy to divide in spring or fall.

yarrow

Achillea 'Coronation Gold'
- Perennial
- 3'
- Summer
- Golden yellow
- Zones 3-10
- Sun
- Sources: ff, ii

Gray foliage; drought tolerant. Vigorous with many bright 3-inch wide blooms. Cut fresh or use for drying.

saucer magnolia

Magnolia x *soulangiana*
- Tree
- 12' in 10 years; up to 30'
- Early spring
- Fragrant
- White with purple
- Zones 4-9
- Sun, light shade
- Sources: e, h, n

Flowers rarely blasted by frost. Can be grown as a multistemmed shrub. Prefers good, moist, deep soil. Good specimen plant.

peach-leafed bellflower

Campanula persicifolia
- Perennial
- 24-36"
- Summer
- Blue
- Zones 3-10
- Sun, part shade

- Sources: e, y, z

Showy clusters of flowers; remove spent flowers for second bloom. Prefers moist soil. 'Alba' is white.

astilbe

Astilbe hyb.
- Perennial
- 18-48"
- Early-late summer
- White to red
- Zones 4-8
- Sun, part shade
- Sources: c, y

Very rewarding plants for shady spots. Attractive, fernlike foliage. Prefers organic, well-drained soil.

bearded iris

Iris spp.
- Perennial
- 16-40"
- Spring, early summer
- White, blue, purple
- Zones 3-10
- Sun
- Sources: f, n, v, ii,

Easy to grow in very well-drained soil. Plant rhizome so top half to one-third is above ground in direction of desired growth. Need to divide only when bloom decreases or to increase stock.

columbine

Aquilegia 'Nora Barlow'
- Perennial
- 24-30"
- Spring, early summer
- Pink with white
- Zones 5-10
- Sun, part shade
- Sources: j, dd

Dependable plant with fully double flowers. Grows best in well-drained soils. Remove any foliage with leaf miner damage (thin white lines in leaves).

shirley poppy

Papaer rhoeas
- Annual
- 18-36"
- Flowers 60 days from sowing
- White to red
- Sun
- Sources: j, v

Elegant, papery flowers followed by hairy pods. Sow seed directly outdoors; self-sows when plant is established. Prefers rich, well-drained soil.

heavenly bamboo

Nandina domestica
- Shrub
- 6-8'
- Late spring, early summer
- Pink buds, white flowers
- Zones 6-9
- Sun to shade
- Sources: e, g, n, y, ff

Not real bamboo. Bright red berries a bonus. Adaptable, tough; can grow under oaks. Thin old stems yearly.

pansy

Viola x *wittrockiana* 'Jolly Joker'
- Annual
- 6-9"
- Spring
- White to purple
- Part shade
- Sources: cc, dd

Outstanding colors. Edible flowers. Start seed indoors 12 weeks before spring frost-free date. Prefers cool weather and moist, rich soil. Deadhead to encourage bloom.

nature's

garden

t

he most powerful element you can add to any garden is water. It's an animating force that fills the landscape with sound, movement, and reflection. A naturalistic pond draws you to the beauty of the plants that grow in and around it. While water attracts birds, butterflies and other wildlife, it also adds serenity to the garden as well as to the gardener's sense of well being.

Waterlilies don't like moving water. Place them at least 5 feet from a waterfall. *Opposite:* Waterlily 'Albert Greenberg'.

t

he Hinz family was faced with a typical suburban small-space backyard in Atlanta, Georgia. The only solution to fitting everything they wanted into the garden was to consider each element as a separate "room."

Designing a landscape with rooms enables gardeners to place "more" into smaller spaces. That is, there are opportunities for planting areas and beds in each room. Rather than borders of shrubs surrounding expanses of lawn, landscape architect Danna Cain divided the backyard into sections, and Tom Hinz eagerly planted them, covering almost every square inch. The features they created include decks, a stone terrace, wildlife area, play yard, and winding paths—all in a suburban setting measuring one-third of an acre.

Danna and Tom wanted the mood of the garden to change as family members and visitors walk from the house to the wild garden. They used a series of steps to achieve this. A multilevel deck goes down to the stone terrace. From here, a narrow stone path winds through the garden to the 15 × 30-foot, slightly kidney-shaped pond. The family can view the pond from the sunroom, making it the key element of the garden.

Their favorite spot in the garden is the bridge, which connects to the stone path. Here, the children can peer into the surface, linger while listening to the musical water, or feed the decorative koi.

If you're considering putting in a pond, check with local authorities before starting. In Atlanta, an unfenced body of water must be less than 18 inches deep. This is sufficient water to support fish (especially in a mild-winter climate, where there's little worry about the water freezing solid) and an assortment of aquatic plants.

The Hinzes used a heavy butyl liner made specifically for artificial ponds and then edged the pond with various river rocks. The unattractive "necklace effect" is avoided; the pond edge undulates and is planted with easy-to-grow Japanese iris and seasonal annuals—New Guinea impatiens in summer and pansies in winter.

Any movement of water, even a small engineered drip, changes the whole ambience of a garden. The Hinzes' two waterfalls spill over a slight slope, adding a gentle voice to the setting.

An added bonus— once built, their pond attracted a variety of wildlife. Lizards, frogs, toads, and chipmunks suddenly showed up, and the bird population increased dramatically to the delight of the family.

PLANTS FOR WILDLIFE

When planning a landscape, choose plants that provide berries, nectar-producing flowers, and some dense shrubs for shelter and cover. Berrying shrubs and trees, such as flowering dogwoods, hollies, beautyberry, and mahonias attract birds.

Add birdhouses, feeders, a birdbath, and nesting shelves to provide safe cover for fledglings. Bird feeders and different seed mixes will draw a wide variety of birds year-round.

Grow some butterfly weed (*Asclepias tuberosa*); it's a good source of food for Monarch caterpillars and provides nectar for adult butterflies. The more habitat elements you incorporate into the landscape, the more wildlife you'll attract.

using water as a focal point

Water sources invite wildlife into the garden.

Childhood memories of frogs, fish, and waving grasses inspired Tom Hinz to work with landscape architect Danna Cain's idea of a pond as the central feature of the new garden. Today, the sounds of water and wildlife fill the urban air—frogs croaking and splashing, fish jumping, and small, beneficial critters scurrying about. The pond made these simple joys possible. And, the resulting colorful backyard provides sanctuary, nature study, play, and entertainment for the whole family. Contact the National Wildlife Federation (703-790-4100) for tips on making your backyard a wildlife habitat.

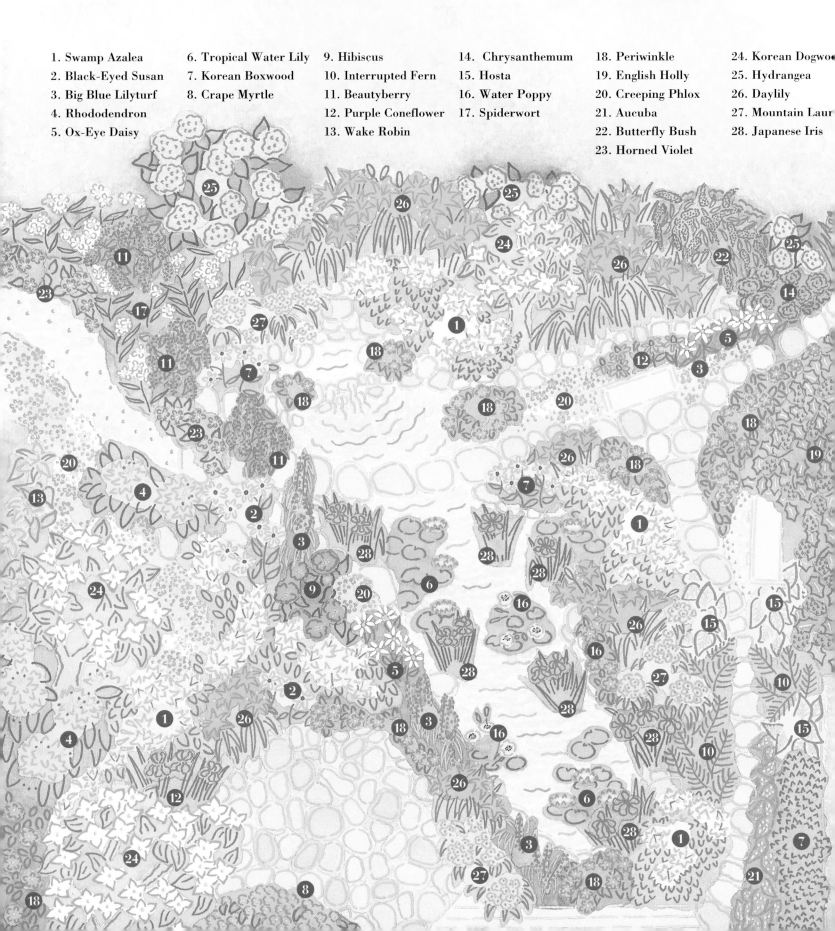

1. Swamp Azalea
2. Black-Eyed Susan
3. Big Blue Lilyturf
4. Rhododendron
5. Ox-Eye Daisy
6. Tropical Water Lily
7. Korean Boxwood
8. Crape Myrtle
9. Hibiscus
10. Interrupted Fern
11. Beautyberry
12. Purple Coneflower
13. Wake Robin
14. Chrysanthemum
15. Hosta
16. Water Poppy
17. Spiderwort
18. Periwinkle
19. English Holly
20. Creeping Phlox
21. Aucuba
22. Butterfly Bush
23. Horned Violet
24. Korean Dogwood
25. Hydrangea
26. Daylily
27. Mountain Laurel
28. Japanese Iris

swamp azalea

Rhododendron vaseyi
- Shrub
- 5-10'
- Late spring
- Fragrant
- Rose
- Zones 4-8
- Shade, part shade
- Sources: e, y, ff

Deciduous. Prefers slightly acid, fertile soil.

black-eyed susan

Rudbeckia fulgida 'Goldsturm'
- Perennial
- 18–24"
- Summer to fall
- Yellow-gold
- Zones 3-10
- Sun
- Sources: b, s, u, y, ff, ii

Daisylike, 4-inch flowers bloom over a long season. Extend season by removing spent flowers. Grows in average soil; needs good drainage.

big blue lilyturf

Liriope muscari 'Variegata'
- Perennial, groundcover
- 8-12"
- Late summer, early fall

- Lavender
- Zones 5-10
- Part shade, sun
- Sources: n, ff, ii

Dependable ground cover. Cream stripes will fade in full sun. Tolerates dry soils. Cut back in early spring.

rhododendron

Rhododendron 'Arsen's Pink'
- Shrub
- 3-4'
- Rose-pink
- Zones 7-9
- Sun, part shade
- Source: y

Grow in organic, acid soil. Shallow-rooted; mulch to conserve moisture. Protect from winter wind and sun.

ox-eye daisy

Leucanthemum vulgare (*Chrysanthemum leucanthemum*)
- Perennial
- 12-24"
- Early summer
- White
- Zones 3-10
- Sun
- Sources: v, z

Forms low mats of deep-green leaves, spreading. Cheery white, yellow-eyed flowers.

tropical water lily

Nymphaea 'Albert Greenberg'
- Perennial, water plant
- 6", spread to 6'
- Summer
- Fragrant
- Pink to yellow

- Zones 8-10
- Sun
- Sources: m, n

Round, floating leaves; gorgeous flowers with multiple hues. Night-blooming; heady fragrance. Needs warmth to bloom.

korean boxwood

Buxus microphylla var. *koreana*
- Shrub, evergreen
- 24-30", spread to 5'
- Foliage plant
- Zones 4-9
- Green shiny leaves
- Sun, part shade
- Sources: a, e, v

Deep rooted; mulch with leaf mold. Protect from drying winds.

crape myrtle

Lagerstroemia hyb.
- Tree
- 15-25'
- Summer, early fall
- White-to-red
- Zones 7-10
- Sun, part shade
- Sources: a, e, n

Attractive peeling bark gives winter interest; can train to a shrub or tree form. Prefers sun, well-drained soil. New varieties are hardier.

hibiscus

Hibiscus rosa-sinensis
'Mollie Cummings'
- Shrub
- 8-15'
- Summer to fall
- Red, pink, orange, yellow
- Zones 9-10
- Sun, part shade
- Sources: e, n, gg, ii

Tropical-looking flowers for big impact; flowers last 1 day. Attractive, glossy leaves. Fast growing.

beautyberry

Callicarpa japonica
- Shrub
- 4-6'
- Summer
- Pink, white
- Zones 5-8
- Sun, part shade
- Sources: a, e, g

Purple berries in fall ('Leucocarpa' has white berries.) Prune to 6 inches high every spring, as it flowers on new wood.

interrupted fern

Osmunda claytonia
- Fern
- 3-4'
- Foliage plant
- Green (yellowish)
- Zones 2-10
- Part shade, sun
- Source: aa

Yellow-green, smooth fronds; deciduous. Grows in moist to dry sites. Needs bright light, ample moisture.

purple coneflower

Echinacea purpurea
- Perennial
- 2-4'
- Summer
- Purple
- Zones 3-10
- Sun
- Sources: j, q, r, v

Low-maintenance native. Flowers attract butterflies; seed heads attract birds in fall and winter.

wake robin

Trillium grandiflorum
- Perennial
- 9-12"
- Spring
- White
- Zones 3-9
- Part shade
- Sources: y, aa, hh

Showy, woodland native. Pure white flowers fade to pink. Easy to grow. Don't dig from wild. Dwarf and double-flowered forms are available.

hosta

Hosta 'Gold Standard'
- Perennial
- 24-36"
- Midsummer
- Pale lavender
- Zones 3-9
- Part shade, shade
- Sources: u, aa

Heart-shaped gold leaves with green edge; gold color deeper in part shade. Forms upright mounds. Grow in rich, moist, organic soil.

chrysanthemum

Dendranthema x *grandiflorum* hyb.(*Chrysanthemum* x *morifolium*)
- Perennial
- 1-6'
- Late summer-frost
- Red
- Zones 4-10
- Source: Buy locally.

Long-lasting color for the fall garden. Hybrids are available in a wide variety of colors and flower shapes. For bushy plant, pinch early and often.

water poppy

Hydrocleys nymphoides
- Perennial (tender)
- 6", spreads 6-9'
- Yellow
- Summer to frost
- Zone 10
- Sun
- Sources: m, n

Handsome, glossy, green-leafed water plant. Cheery flowers with purple centers bloom continuously.

spiderwort

Tradescantia virginiana
- Perennial
- 18–36″
- Late spring–fall
- White, pink, or purple
- Zones 5-10
- Sun, Part shade
- Sources: q, y

Easy-to-grow, pretty, sprawling plant; good background plant. Spreads. Long blooming. Many named varieties.

periwinkle

Vinca minor
- Perennial
- 6″
- Early spring
- Lavender-purple
- Zones 4-7
- Sun, shade
- Sources: b, s, gg

Often called myrtle. Nice looking, glossy-leafed, evergreen groundcover. Spreads well. Can be a pest in good soil/sun; contain with edging.

english holly

Ilex aquifolium
- Shrub, evergreen
- 30-50′, generally
- Red fruit
- Fall, winter
- Zones 6-9
- Part shade, sun
- Sources: a, e, y

Shiny, dark green, spiny leaves on a dense tree-like shrub. Dioecious; need male and female tree for berry production (on female only). Easy, low-maintenance plant.

creeping phlox

Phlox stolonifera hyb.
- Perennial
- 6″
- Spring
- White to purple
- Zones 4–9
- Sun, part-shade
- Sources: g, y

Good groundcover forming dense mats. Requires well-drained soil. Cut back right after flowering.

aucuba

Aucuba japonica
- Shrub
- 6-10′, generally
- Very early spring
- Purple
- Zones 7-10
- Shade
- Sources: a, e, n

Also known as Japanese laurel. Tough plant for deep shade in warm areas. Variegated forms brighten dark areas of the garden.

butterfly bush

Buddleia davidii
- Shrub
- 5-10′
- Summer to frost
- Fragrant
- White to purple
- Zones 5-9

- Sun, part shade
- Sources: a, e, f, n

Attracts butterflies; deadhead spent flowers for continuous bloom. Prefers well-drained soil, full sun. For best flowering, cut plant down to ground level in early spring.

horned violet

Viola cornuta
- Perennial
- 6-12″
- Early spring
- Fragrant
- Shades of purple
- Zones 6-10
- Part shade, sun
- Sources: t, cc, dd

Tidy plant; does well in moist, organic soil; mulch in summer. Cut back after bloom.

korean dogwood

Cornus kousa
- Tree, deciduous
- 20-30′, equal spread
- Late spring, early summer
- White (bracts)
- Zones 5-8
- Part shade, sun
- Sources: g, n, y

Also known as kousa dogwood. Four-season tree with long flowering and foliage periods. Showy white "flowers" (bracts), reddish fruit, brown mosaic bark, good winter structure.

hydrangea

Hydrangea macrophylla
'Nikko Blue'
- Shrub
- 6'
- Summer
- Pink/blue, blue/pink
- Zones 6-9
- Sun, part shade
- Sources: a, e, n, gg

Big, "mop-head" flowers;
borne on a rounded shrub.
Tough plant. Grow in acid soil
for best, deep-blue flowers.

mountain laurel

Kalmia latifolia
- Shrub, evergreen
- 7-15'
- Late spring, early summer
- White to rose
- Zones 4-9
- Sun to shade
- Sources: a, j, jj

Easy-to-grow, robust shrub for
shade, natural, or woodland
gardens. Needs moist, well-
drained, acid soil. Mulch well.

daylily

Hemerocallis
'Raspberry Frolic'
- Perennial
- 30"
- Spring, reblooms
- Fragrant
- Rosy lavender
- Zones 3-10
- Sun, part shade
- Sources: l, n

Durable plant. Lightly scented.
Unlike other daylilies, flowers
last over 16 hours. New buds
open over a period of weeks.

japanese iris

Iris ensata hyb.
- Perennial
- 2-3'
- Summer
- White to purple
- Zones 5-10
- Sun, part shade
- Sources: e, n, ii

Elegant sword-shaped foliage
remains after blooms. Prefers
very moist soils or shallow
water. Divide every 3 years in
fall to keep plant vigorous.

dried flower garden

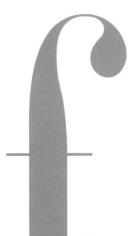reshly cut flowers generally are short-lived. However, you can prolong the enjoy-ment of your garden by using dried flowers in arrange-ments. With new techniques, most flowers can be preserved, but this takes a lot of time and effort. Everlastings are a select group of annuals and peren-nials that may be cut from the garden and simply hung upside down to air dry. Once dried, they last for years, providing colorful bouquets, wreaths, or swags.

Flowers can dry within a week in a warm, well ventilated room. *Opposite*: Plumed cockscomb.

easy-to-grow dried flowers

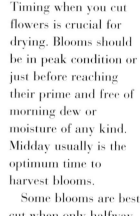

the joy of an everlasting garden is watching flowers from the moment they are planted until they are assembled into long-lived arrangements.

Everlastings are a group of perennnials and annuals particularly suited to air drying without losing their forms or colors. Many of these flowers turn papery and dry in the garden.

Annual everlastings are among the easiest of flowers to grow from seed. For the earliest flowering, start them indoors, in pots, four to six weeks before transplanting them into the garden. Or, sow the seed directly in the garden after the last frost in spring.

The drying process is simple. You can cut most everlastings, strip the leaves and stems, then secure them in small bunches with rubber bands. Hang the bunches upside down in a dark, dry, warm spot—an attic is perfect, but a closet or garage will do. If you're in an area with high humidity, drying flowers can be challenging. For good results, dry them in a room where you keep a dehumidifier.

It's best to let grasses and small or delicate flowers dry flat. Place them on wire screens raised at least 6 inches above the floor so air can circulate around the blooms. In two to three weeks, most flowers will be ready to use in bouquets, wreaths, or other arrangements.

And, you can dry the foliage of some plants, including many herbs, to use in arrangements or craft projects. The silvery foliage of the artemisias, including 'Silver King' and 'Silver Mound', adds an intriguing textural component to an arrangement. Children love lamb's ears (*Stachys byzantina*), with their furry silver leaves, which are fun to stroke whether they're fresh or dried.

Cut sweet Annie (*Artemisia annua*) and tie it to a wreath form while it's still green: the fragrance is fresh and woodsy. Wear gloves when handling it: some people are sensitive to volatile oils in this plant. The aroma of culinary sage adds a hint of spiciness to a wreath.

Look at the seed pods of other plants to use in dried arrangements. The prickly, bluish heads of globe thistle (*Echinops ritro*) and the ghostly sea hollies (*Eryngium* spp.) are striking.

PRIME-TIME HARVEST

Timing when you cut flowers is crucial for drying. Blooms should be in peak condition or just before reaching their prime and free of morning dew or moisture of any kind. Midday usually is the optimum time to harvest blooms.

Some blooms are best cut when only halfway open, as they will continue to mature after being cut. These include ageratum, bachelor's-button, larkspur, strawflower, peonies, roses, statice, baby's breath, and lamb's ears. Wait until the blooms fully open (but before they start browning) to cut yarrow, allium, celosia, purple coneflower, sage, showy sunray, rudbeckia, and tansy.

The brightly-colored, plumed flower heads of cockscomb air dry easily. *Opposite:* Garden overview.

For her garden of *everlasting* and beautiful flowers,

Katherine Macy has a number of narrow, 4-foot wide borders. She gives free-form clumps of plants ample space so the border not only has a pleasing appearance, but the plants also have enough room to grow and mature. Gardening on the north shore of Long Island, New York, Katherine used to have a regular cutting garden until she discovered the long-lasting beauty of dried flowers. Now her gardens are filled with flowers she can dry and use in numerous arrangements. And, her attic is filled with remembrances of her summer garden rather than dusty mementos of the past.

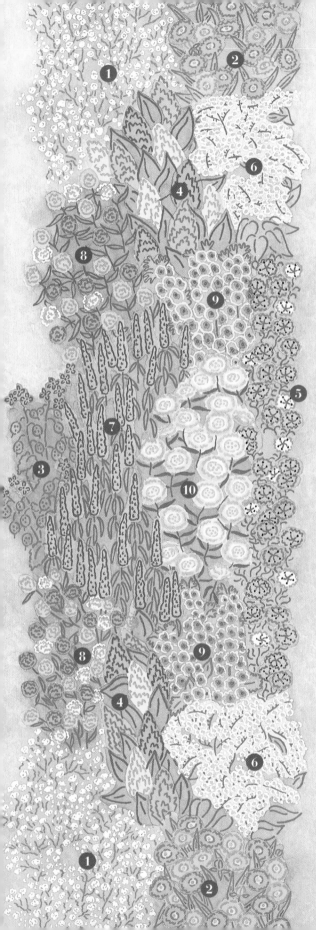

strawflower

Helichrysum bracteatum
- Annual
- 24-60"
- Summer
- Yellow/orange with accents
- Sun
- Source: f

Unattractive foliage; best in a cutting garden. Pick before bloom opens; hang upside down to dry. Sow seed directly outdoors.

baby's breath

Gypsophila paniculata 'Compacta Plena'
- Perennial
- 12-24"
- Summer
- White
- Zones 3-10
- Sun

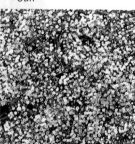

- Sources: c, e

Numerous tiny flowers look like fireworks. Good flower to cut fresh or to dry. Plant it where you want it to live; the deep tap root doesn't transplant well.

plumed cockscomb

Celosia argentea var. *cristata* 'Sparkler Hybri'
- Annual
- 8-36"
- Summer-frost

- Yellow to purple
- Sun
- Sources: j, v, cc

Start seed indoors; transplant outdoors after last spring frost. Tolerates dry soil; thrives in heat. Long lasting flowers.

money plant

Lunaria annua
- Biennial
- 30-36"
- Purple, white
- Zones 5-9
- Sun, part shade
- Source: b

Blooms second year from seed; leave some seed pods on plant, so it can self-sow. For indoor use, peel off brown papery shell to reveal silvery, disclike seed pods.

1. Baby's Breath
2. Strawflower
3. Money Plant
4. Plumed Cockscomb
5. Love-in-a-Mist
6. German Statice
7. Mealy-Cup Sage
8. Globe Amaranth
9. Bells-of-Ireland
10. Showy Sunray

love-in-a-mist

Nigella damascena
'Specialty Mix'
- Annual
- 12-18"
- Summer
- White to purple
- Sun
- Sources: k, r, t

Sow seed outdoors every 3 weeks. Decorative seed pods.

mealy-cup sage

Salvia farinacea
'Victoria'
- Annual
- 18-24"
- Summer-fall
- Deep blue

- Sun
- Source: dd

Prolific bloomer; excellent for border, bedding, and cutting gardens. Great for fresh or dried bouquets. Needs well-drained, nutrient-laden soil.

german statice

Goniolimon tataricum
(Limonium tataricum)
- Perennial
- 18-24"
- Summer
- Pink
- Zones 3-10
- Sun
- Sources: b, f, j, r, s, v

Tiny pink flowers. Showy white calyx and silvery-white foliage attractive even after flowering. Resembles baby's breath.

globe amaranth

Gomphrena globosa
- Annual
- 6-24"
- Summer
- White to purple
- Sun
- Sources: b, s

Slow to grow from seed; start indoors 8 weeks before last frost date. Prefers warm weather. Hang upside down to dry.

bells-of-ireland

Moluccella laevis
- Annual
- 24-30"
- Summer
- Green "bells"
- Sun, part shade
- Source: b

Stately flower spikes; green "flowers" dry to straw color.

showy sunray

Helipterum splendidum
- Annual
- 24"
- Summer
- White, chamois, pink
- Sun
- Source: i

Cut flower just before it opens; can be used fresh or air dried. Hang upside down to dry. Sow seed directly in the garden.

islands
of color

m

ulticolor islands of flowers almost seem to float in a blue-green sea of grassy lawn; some stand alone, while others conjoin. Walk around a bend and you'll come upon an entirely different scene. The massive beds of trees, shrubs, and perennials, which were designed to be seen and enjoyed from a distance, also can be viewed close-up. Take pleasure in focusing on a flower that catches your eye from afar.

Cool-toned phlox and queen-of-the-prairie partner well with bold yarrow. *Opposite*: Cranesbill.

Yarrow is a carefree perennial that makes a good dried flower. *Opposite:* Overview of garden.

in this rural Pennsylvania garden, most of the island beds exhibit a casual symmetry; the same shrub or perennial anchors the center and sides. Such repetition adds visual strength to the beds, even though the color theme is a blend of soft hues such as blue, pink, and light yellow. White flowers are used as a neutralizing element between colors, as is the silvery foliage of butterfly bush and artemisia.

Boldly colored flowers ensure notice from a distance. Some have an added bonus, such as the flaming red Asiatic lily that also attracts hummingbirds. It makes a wonderful accent planted anywhere.

When planning a large island bed, include some small trees or shrubs to provide height and scale for the plantings. Here, azaleas and butterfly bushes offer mass and height during the growing season and give a woody presence throughout winter.

Ornamental grasses, such as any of the large miscanthus, add height. They draw interest year-round; they're unattractive only for several weeks after they're cut down. You also can create structure with woody plants, such as oakleaf hydrangea, weeping cherry, Frasier fir, or Harry Lauder's walking stick (*Corylus avellana* 'Contorta'), a uniquely gnarled and contorted form of hazelnut.

Experiment with themes and designs in island beds. Focal-point possibilities include a bed with a birdbath, fountain, or garden seat in the center. Consider a raised bed using local stones to create a rock or succulent garden. Or, feature ornamental grasses, herbs, fragrant plants, seasonal bulbs, or any other plant group or type that you love. Vary the beds by soil type. For example, have one for acid-loving plants such as azaleas, rhododendrons, and heathers.

In large island beds, it's helpful to add paths, so you can reach all the plants without walking through the garden and compacting the soil. Compacted soil suffocates the roots, slowly killing the plants.

Island beds provide the opportunity to remedy soil problems. Improve any soil by adding organic matter. If you add a lot of organic matter, you'll have an instant raised bed. It will be all the more arresting, with better growing conditions and drainage.

Laying Out A Bed

Use a garden hose to lay out the perimeter of the island. Walk around the bed and adjust the hose until you're satisfied with the shape from all perspectives. Come back the next day and look at the bed with a fresh eye. Once you're satisfied, use lime to mark the edge. Or, you can simply mow around the edge of the bed to mark its boundaries.

The best time to start a new bed is in the fall so it has all winter to get ready for spring planting. To kill the existing grass, cover it with 15 to 20 sheets of wet newspaper. Cover that with 6 to 8 inches of organic matter: straw, hay, manure, or compost. By spring, the organic matter will have broken down the grass and newspaper, and then you'll have a "no-dig" bed.

view **islands** from near or far

In a yard with a vista view, large-scale plantings are

a must; small plantings would be totally lost. In Pamela Gladding's Pennsylvania backyard, pine woods stretch into the distance, and mountains accent the view. She designed four large island beds, up to 15 feet wide by 100 feet long, with organic shapes to blend with the mountains and pond.

Gladding, an artist, wants her island beds to be enjoyed from the back porch. She "paints" them, using bold strokes: large clumps of perennials, shrubs, trees, and some added surprises— "exclamation point" plants such as Asiatic lilies. These borders are bold enough for this setting.

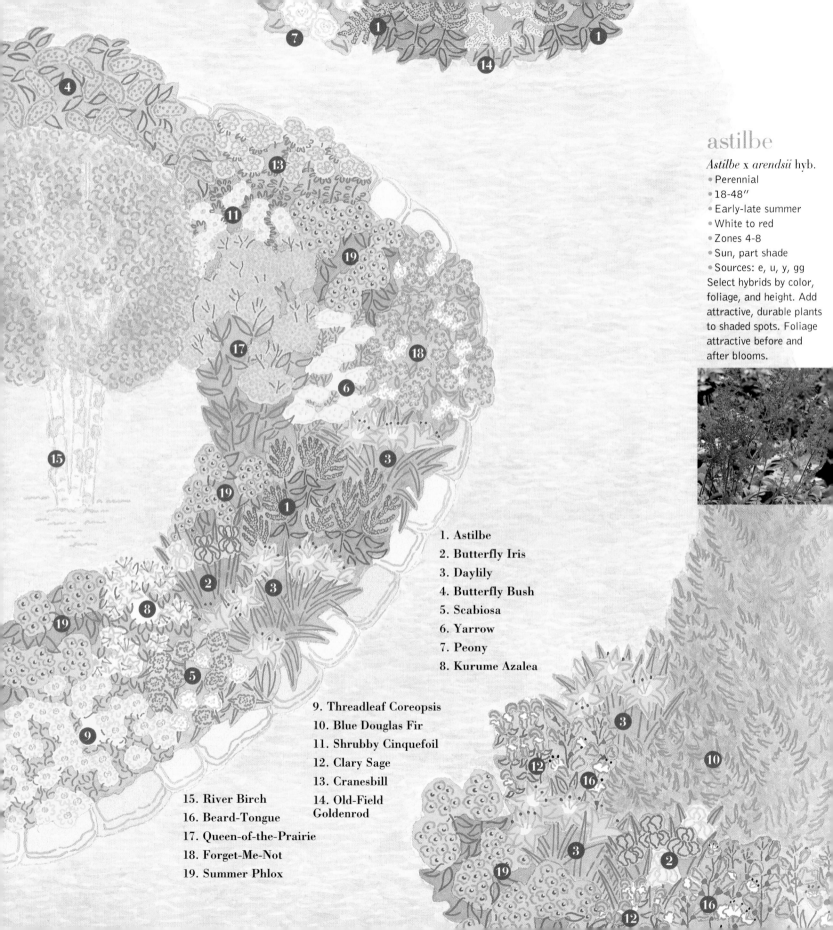

astilbe

Astilbe x *arendsii* hyb.
- Perennial
- 18-48"
- Early-late summer
- White to red
- Zones 4-8
- Sun, part shade
- Sources: e, u, y, gg

Select hybrids by color, foliage, and height. Add attractive, durable plants to shaded spots. Foliage attractive before and after blooms.

1. Astilbe
2. Butterfly Iris
3. Daylily
4. Butterfly Bush
5. Scabiosa
6. Yarrow
7. Peony
8. Kurume Azalea

9. Threadleaf Coreopsis
10. Blue Douglas Fir
11. Shrubby Cinquefoil
12. Clary Sage
13. Cranesbill
14. Old-Field Goldenrod

15. River Birch
16. Beard-Tongue
17. Queen-of-the-Prairie
18. Forget-Me-Not
19. Summer Phlox

butterfly iris

Iris spuria
- Perennial
- 2-5'
- Early summer
- White, yellow, purple
- Zones 4-9
- Sun
- Source: e

Long-lasting flowers resemble butterflies. Most trouble-free iris. Drought tolerant. Summer dormant.

daylily

Hemerocallis hyb.
- Perennial
- 1-4'
- Late spring to fall
- White to burgundy
- Zones 3-10
- Sun, part shade
- Sources: b, s, y

Durable, long-blooming garden favorites. Prefer deep, rich, well-drained soil. Divide every 3 years or when blooms are less numerous. Interplant with tulips or daffodils.

butterfly bush

Buddleia davidii 'Nanho Blue'
- Shrub
- 3-5'
- Summer
- Mauve blue with orange "eye"

- Zones 5-9
- Sun
- Sources: a, u, y

Small-growing, handsome shrub attracts butterflies. Can be grown in container. Cut down to ground level in spring; blooms on new wood. Deadhead spent flowers for rebloom.

scabiosa

Scabiosa caucasica hyb.
- Perennial
- 18-30"
- Summer-late summer
- Blue to white
- Zones 3-10
- Sun
- Sources: e, gg, ii

Many excellent named hybrids; 2-to 3-inch, flat flowers. Deadhead for long-lasting bloom.

yarrow

Achillea 'Moonshine'
- Perennial
- 24"
- Summer
- Yellow
- Zones 4-10
- Sun
- Source: e

Silvery-gray leaves; 3- to 4-inch, sulfur-yellow flowers. Grows well in dry, sunny areas. Excellent flower for cutting and drying.

peony

Paeonia lactiflora 'Top Brass'
- Perennial
- 18-42"
- Spring
- Fragrant
- White
- Zones 2-10
- Sources: gg, ii

Spectacular garden favorite; handsome foliage. Rich perfume. Needs deep, rich soil and full sun.

kurume azalea

Rhododendron
Kurume hyb.
- Shrub
- 5-7'
- Late spring
- Pink to scarlet
- Zones 5-8
- Shade, part shade
- Sources: e, y, ff

Small leaves; compact habit. May be shaped.

threadleaf coreopsis

Coreopsis verticillata
'Zagreb'
- Perennial
- 10-12"
- Summer-fall
- Yellow
- Zones 3-10
- Sun
- Sources: e, g, gg

Dwarf form (though not always reliably so) with long season of bloom; fernlike foliage. Drought resistant.

blue douglas fir

Pseudotsuga menziesii
'Glauca'
- Tree, evergreen
- 40-80', spread to 20'
- Bluish-green foliage
- Zones 4-7
- Sun

- Sources: g, ff

Very ornamental; use as a specimen tree or in mass planting. Prefers well-drained, moist soil. Don't plant in windy, exposed spots.

shrubby cinquefoil

Potentilla fruticosa
'Yellow Bird'
- Shrub
- 1-4'
- Summer to frost
- Yellow
- Zones 2-7
- Sun, part shade
- Sources: e, y

Prefers rich, moist, well-drained soil. Cut one-third of canes in late winter to maintain vigor.

clary sage

Salvia sclarea
- Biennial
- 3-5'
- Spring, summer
- Fragrant
- White and blue
- Zones 5-9
- Sun
- Sources: r, f, v

Popular, attractive herb; large leaves and 1-inch flowers with aromatic, medicinal smell. Remains showy for weeks. Plants release fragrance after a rain. Self-sows.

cranesbill

Geranium sanguineum
var. *striatum*
- Perennial
- 9-18"
- Late spring, summer
- Pale pink, dark veins
- Zones 4-10
- Sun, part shade
- Sources: e, ii, gg

Nice, low-growing mounds of attractive, divided leaves. Easy to grow in well-drained soils. Deadhead for even longer bloom.

old-field goldenrod

Solidago nemoralis
- Perennial
- 18-36"
- Midsummer to fall
- Yellow
- Zones 4-9
- Sun, part shade
- Source: f

Attractive, durable, long blooming. Many new hybrids. Doesn't cause hay fever.

river birch

Betula nigra 'Heritage'
- Tree
- 40-60'
- Zones 4-9
- Sun, part shade
- Sources: e, n, ii

Very vigorous selection (patented variety) with rugged, peeling bark, ranging from light brown to cream and brown catkins. Pest resistant. Does best in moist soils.

beard-tongue

Penstemon hyb.
- Perennial
- 1-4'
- Summer
- White to red
- Zones 3-10
- Sun
- Sources: q, u, bb

Very attractive, drought tolerant native plant. Requires sun and perfect drainage. Good hybrids. 'Husker's Red' is choice plant in any border.

forget-me-not

Myosotis sylvatica
- Biennial
- 6-18"
- Spring
- Blue to white
- Zones 5-9
- Part shade
- Sources: s, dd, gg

Classic spring planting with bulbs. Prefers cool weather. Self-sows under shrubs and at woodland edges. Or, sow seed in the garden in spring.

queen-of-the-prairie

Filipendula rubra
- Perennial
- 6-8'
- Summer
- Pink
- Zones 3-9
- Sun, part shade
- Sources: ff, ii

Midwest native. Forms massive stands. Grows best in moist, cool areas. Makes a good cut flower.

summer phlox

Phlox paniculata
'Eva Cullum'
- Perennial
- 2-3'
- Summer-early fall
- Fragrant
- Pink, with dark pink eye
- Zones 3-9
- Sun
- Sources: e, y, ff, gg, ii

Needs deep, rich soil. Water during drought. Thin to 6 stems in spring for strong stems. Deadhead.

four season garden

Changing the scenery with the seasons is what this exuberant Midwest garden is all about. Helaine Mackey experiments with the plantings in her Clarksville, Missouri, garden. As she learns about new and different plants, she introduces them into her garden. Helaine focuses on plants with multiseason interest—whether the attraction is flowers, foliage, fruit, stems, texture, or form.

An old wicker chair adds sculptural flair as plants grow through it in summer. *Opposite*: Bee balm.

h

elaine Mackey has strong feelings about her garden, planting only what she wants. While her choices may be subject to change, she's unwavering about roses.

She won't grow them because, for her, they're too much work.

Her 180 × 132-foot garden allows ample room for experimenting and indulging her garden fantasies. Pathways curve through her two large beds that are set off and separated by a well-trimmed lawn. Austrian and white pines serve as the backdrop for beds of daylilies, coneflowers, and other perennials. A huge, old maple tree, blue spruce, yellow and red twig dogwood, and lilacs give the garden a sense of structure.

Vintage wicker chairs provide seating, and an old, weathered metal well cap and a tiny playhouse add more structure.

Current favorites always define the beds. One year Helaine was smitten by yellow daylilies, another she was taken with large leaves and foliage plants such as hostas. In other years, hollyhocks, leatherleaf viburnum, and bearded iris struck her fancy. Her latest infatuations include daylilies, Asiatic lilies, and pearl petunias.

A color preference or combinations of color sometimes suggest choices—for a few years, lemon yellow and pink reigned supreme.

plant lover's all-season garden

Despite her predilection for change, Helaine sticks to some of the basics of garden design. If you want to create visual impact in the garden, she advises, start with the background. Consider the trees, walls, fences, and buildings and then add color. There's a greater effect when you plant in groups of three, five or seven—large drifts of color rather than emphasis on single plants. To energize the garden, experiment with unpredictable combinations, such as pairing feathery baby's-breath with upright hollyhocks.

Helaine stresses the importance of pathways.

A well-laid out path will draw you to the focal point of the garden. Paths also help set the style of the garden. Old bricks or fieldstones suit a country garden well. Wood chips, pine straw, or packed earth nicely fit a woodland or wildflower garden.

Structures and accents are strong focal points, when used sparingly. Place birdbaths, sundials, or pink flamingos judiciously.

SIMPLIFY MAINTENANCE
Mulching saves time and energy. Use a heavy spring mulch around perennials. Start with a few layers of newspaper, add 12 inches of straw, then a topdressing of shredded bark. This creates an environment that holds in moisture, requires little or no watering, and doesn't give weeds a chance to grow. Only annuals and potted plants need scheduled watering.

After frost, Helaine mows all the perennials to the ground. This time-saving technique also provides winter cover for the beds. As an alternative, you can compost the cut material and give the beds a layer of finished compost leaf mold. Either way, this allows the spring bulbs, such as daffodils, to show off without competing with old foliage.

Use color and structures to create visual interest.

As she was designing her Clarksville, Missouri, garden, Helaine Mackey found the barren ground cried out for plants and structure. To start the daunting task of creating beds where nothing existed, Helaine placed milk cans where she thought the structural elements of the new garden should be. This technique helped to guide her to the right balance of trees, beds, lawn, and garden sculptures. This type of real-world technique makes visualizing a two-dimensional plan much easier. And, by giving a sense of scale, it helps avoid lots of labor-intensive errors in the process.

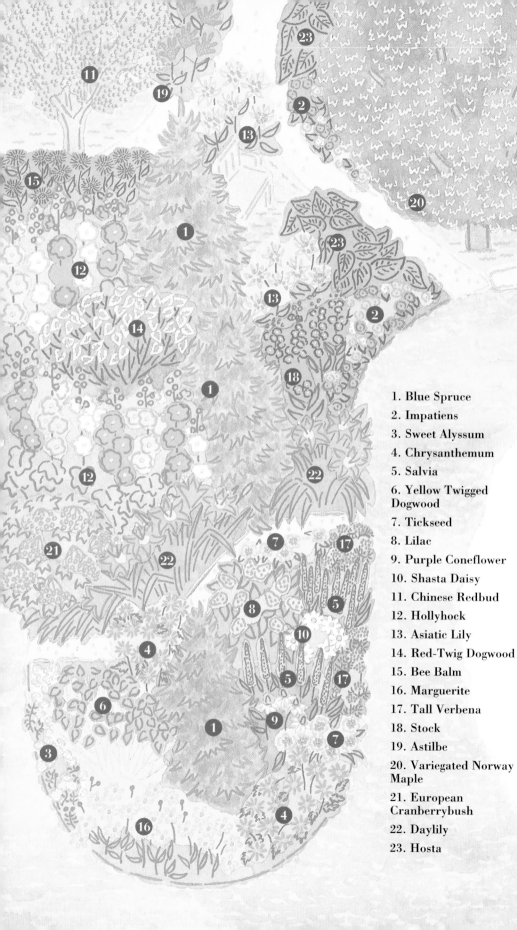

1. Blue Spruce
2. Impatiens
3. Sweet Alyssum
4. Chrysanthemum
5. Salvia
6. Yellow Twigged Dogwood
7. Tickseed
8. Lilac
9. Purple Coneflower
10. Shasta Daisy
11. Chinese Redbud
12. Hollyhock
13. Asiatic Lily
14. Red-Twig Dogwood
15. Bee Balm
16. Marguerite
17. Tall Verbena
18. Stock
19. Astilbe
20. Variegated Norway Maple
21. European Cranberrybush
22. Daylily
23. Hosta

impatiens

Impatiens walleriana hyb.
- Annual
- 12-24"
- Summer-frost
- White to purple
- Part shade, shade
- Sources: b, s, dd

Extremely easy, colorful plants provide nonstop flowering in shade; quick color for tough spots. Prefers moist soil.

blue spruce

Picea pungens 'Glauca'
- Tree, evergreen
- 30-60', spread to 20'
- Silvery-blue foliage
- Zones 2-8
- Sun
- Sources: g, y dd

Choose plant by foliage color. Group with other plants in the garden rather than as front-yard specimen. Drought tolerant once established; water it well for 2 years if there's insufficient rainfall.

sweet alyssum

Lobularia maritima
- Annual
- 2-12", spread to 10"
- Summer-frost
- Fragrant
- White
- Sun, part shade
- Sources: b, s, dd

Very useful plant as edging, groundcover, filler, or living mulch in pots. Honey-scented; white varieties most fragrant. Easy to grow from seed; self-sows.

chrysanthemum

Dendranthema x
grandiflora 'Centerpiece'
- Perennial
- 2-4'
- Early fall to frost
- Pale pink with yellow
- Zones 4-10
- Sun
- Source: Buy locally

Good late-season color;
many shapes available.

salvia

Salvia 'Indigo Spires'
- Perennial
- 30-36"
- Summer-fall
- Purple
- Zones 7-10
- Sun, part shade
- Sources: o, u, ff, jj

Bushy hybrid; long, arching
flower stalks from summer
to frost. An excellent cut
flower; can be air dried.
Well worth growing as an
annual in colder areas.

yellow-twigged dogwood

Cornus stolonifera
'Flaviramea'
(*C. sericea*)
- Shrub
- 7-9', spread to 10'

- Late spring
- White
- Zones 2-8
- Sun
- Sources: a, e, ff

Yellow twig winter
color requires careful
placement; use in shrub
border. Prefers moist
soil. Prune every few
years to maintain
vibrant color. Watch for
canker on bark.

tickseed

Coreopsis lanceolata
hyb.
- Perennial
- 1-2'
- Early summer-summer
- Yellow
- Zones 4-10
- Sources: f, v, cc

Long-flowering, useful
native plant. Daisylike
flowers; deadhead to
prevent self-sowing.
Named cultivars are
superior to species.

lilac

Syringa meyeri
- Shrub
- 4-8'
- Late spring, early
  summer
- Fragrant
- Violet-purple
- Zones 3-7
- Sun
- Sources: a, e, y, ii

Many flowers; lightly
fragrant; may rebloom.
Compact shrubs need
little maintenance. Plant
in front of evergreens.
'Palibin' only 5 feet tall.

purple coneflower

Echinacea purpurea
'Magnus'
- Perennial
- 2-4'
- Summer-early fall
- Pink-purple
- Zones 4-10

- Sun
- Sources: b, e, dd

Flat-petaled version of
popular native species.
"Perennial Plant of the
Year" (1998). Easy to
grow in average soil. A
good addition to any
mixed border.

shasta daisy

Leuchanthemum x
superbum
(*Chrysanthemum* x
superbum)
- Perennial
- 1-3'
- Early summer-fall
- White
- Zones 5-10
- Sun, part shade
- Sources: cc, ii, gg

Old favorite with long-
lasting color. Easy to
grow; divide every few
years. Good cut flower.

chinese redbud

Cercis chinensis
- Shrub
- 10-15'
- Late winter,
  early spring
- Rosy-purple
- Zones 6-9
- Sun, part shade
- Sources: a, e, g, n, ff

Spectacular in flower.
Particularly good in the
South. Prefers moist,
well-drained soil.

hollyhock

Alcea rosea
'Outhouse Hollyhocks'
- Biennial
- 6-10'
- Summer
- White to purple
- Sun
- Sources: v, ii, cc, t

Big, 3-inch flowers on upright, hairy stems. Many colors and forms available. Reseeds, so may seem perennial.

asiatic lily

Lilium 'Willowwood'
- Bulb
- 4-6'
- Summer
- Yellow with brown
- Zones 4-9
- Sun, part shade
- Sources: d, n, ii

Asiatic lilies are perennial, low-maintenance bulbs. Flowers face outward and upward. Plant in groups. Shade roots.

red-twig dogwood

Cornus alba 'Westonbirt'
- Shrub
- 7-9', spread to 10'
- Late spring
- White
- Zones 2-7

- Sun
- Source: e

Use massed or in shrub border. Broadly variegated leaves. Red twigs are striking against snow in winter. Prune in early spring; most vibrant color is on new wood. Grows best in moist soils.

bee balm

Monarda didyma
- Perennial
- 30-36"
- Summer
- Fragrant
- Red to white
- Zones 4-10
- Sun, part shade
- Sources: f, v, aa, jj

Native plant known as Oswego tea. Dark green, aromatic leaves. Good in meadow. Roots can run. Edible flowers; leaves used to make tea.

marguerite

Argyranthemum frutescens
(*Chrysanthemum frutescens*)
- Annual
- 24-30"
- Summer
- Yellow, white
- Sun
- Sources: e, o

Attractive, aromatic gray-green foliage. Pinch back early for sturdy growth. Nice container plant. Needs well-drained soil.

tall verbena

Verbena bonariensis
- Perennial
- 3-6'
- Summer-early fall
- Purple
- Fragrant

- Zones 7-11
- Sun
- Sources: f, s, q, z

Wonderful, wiry stems topped with small fragrant flowers. Put in front of border for a "veil" effect. Great in mass plantings. Self-sows even in cold winter areas. Should be in every garden.

stock

Matthiola incana hyb.
- Biennial (treat as annual)
- 12-30"
- Spring
- Fragrant
- White to purple
- Sun
- Sources: s, cc, dd

Clove scented. Treat as an annual. Start seed very early outdoors. Likes cool weather.

astilbe

Astilbe chinensis 'Veronica Klose'
- Perennial
- 12-20"
- Summer, late summer
- Rose-purple
- Zones 4-8
- Sun, part shade
- Sources: y, aa

Attractive lacy-green foliage; long-lasting flowers. Prefers moist, organic soil. Attractive in mass plantings or in mixed borders.

variegated norway maple

Acer platanoides hyb.
- Tree
- 40-50'
- Foliage
- Green leaves with white, yellow variegations
- Zones 3-7
- Sun
- Sources: a, h

Large, quick-growing tree. Select leaf color of choice. Easy to grow in average soil.

daylily

Hemerocallis x hyb.
- Perennial
- 1-4'
- Spring, fall
- Burgundy to white
- Zones 3-10
- Sun, part shade
- Sources: b, s, y

Durable, long-blooming favorites. Prefer deep, rich, well-drained soil. Divide every 3 to 5 years. Interplant with spring bulbs.

european cranberrrybush

Viburnum opulus 'Xanthocarpa'
- Shrub
- 8-10'
- Late spring, early summer
- White
- Zones 4-8
- Sun, part shade
- Source: i

Three-season shrub; pale green leaves, yellow fruit in fall. Likes moist soil. Good specimen plant.

hosta

Hosta 'Sum and Substance'
- Perennial
- 30"
- Late summer
- Lavender
- Zones 3-9
- Sun, part shade
- Sources: u, y, aa

One of the best hostas; tough, glossy, textured, heart-shaped leaves. Tolerates more sun than most hostas; leaf color is deeper in the shade.

scented

garden

a country-in-the-city garden offers a fun and magical retreat with gently curving paths, quaint fences, lively flowers, and fragrant herbs. Here, the cares of urban existence fade away as fragrant air transports you to a new place. While wandering about, you notice the aroma of some plants as you brush past them; others reveal their scents only at night, while some continually perfume the air.

creating the scented garden

t his San Francisco backyard garden suffered years of neglect. It underwent a transformation when owner Jeanne Rose, an herbalist with an interest in aroma-therapy, enlisted the help of neighbor and landscape architect Chris Jacobson to create a new garden.

Jeanne had two prerequisites for the garden: She wanted to include as many plants with healing scents as possible, and she needed space for her two large dogs to run and play without destroying the garden. She wanted the garden to be fresh and unmanicured—a country garden in the midst of the city.

The plan includes a core 5 × 5-foot "meadow"—a riotous cornucopia of color and scent. An oval path around the meadow allows room for the dogs to run. Part of the path is old brick salvaged from demolished buildings; the rest is poured concrete covered with an assortment of shells, stones, and even fragments of old bottles. A "higgledy-piggledy" fence assembled from oddball cedar pieces serves as a low-level barrier to protect the garden from the dogs. The texture and jagged quality ensure a genuine country feeling.

The importance of scent influenced most of Jeanne's plant selection.

One of the most fragrant plants in her garden is lemon verbena. Although not as showy as old-fashioned garden verbena, its fragrance makes up for any visual deficit. Five varieties of lavender grow in a brick circle at the edge of the meadow. Bathed in sunshine, this spot stays rather dry—perfect conditions for any Mediterranean herbs such as thyme, rosemary, and oregano.

Jeanne says that working with scented plants requires several general guidelines. Place such plants near paths so visitors strolling by will gently brush them and release the scent of their leaves. Rosemary, pineapple sage, scented geraniums, thyme, and sage are some of the best herbs for this use. Any of the mints, along with lemon balm, are very fragrant, but grow them in containers to keep them within bounds.

Spring-blooming bulbs—many daffodils, tulips, and hyacinths—add sweetness to the garden early in the season. Plant some in window boxes or other areas so you don't have to bend down to catch their aromas.

SCENTS ON A BREEZE

You can catch the scents of many plants from a distance; they drift out to meet you or sometimes seem to assault you. Shrubs, such as mock orange, *Viburnum carlesii, Daphne caucasica,* gardenia, and lilac, have scents noticeable from some distance.

Boxwood and privet also are quite fragrant on sunny, warm days, though their aromas are not enjoyed by everyone. Wisteria, sweet autumn clematis, and Carolina jessamine all produce sweet scents.

Old roses look spectacular in any garden and smell even better. Locate them where the breeze can catch their scent and carry it through a nearby open window.

Despite their wee size, lily-of-the-valley blooms are very aromatic, generously perfuming the air around them.

Eclectic treasures, heady scents, and room for dogs

to run—what more could anyone want? Like many San Francisco residences, Jeanne Rose's three-story Victorian brownstone is close to her neighbors, but you're unaware of the proximity when you step into her cozy, 25 × 70-foot backyard. Birds singing, wind chimes tinkling, and scents wafting through the air overtake street noises. Jeanne, an herbalist, says that being in her garden and breathing deeply amounts to aromatherapy. "A garden must be filled with healing scents to promote well being," she says. "And, the dogs can be out there with me, but they can't hurt the garden."

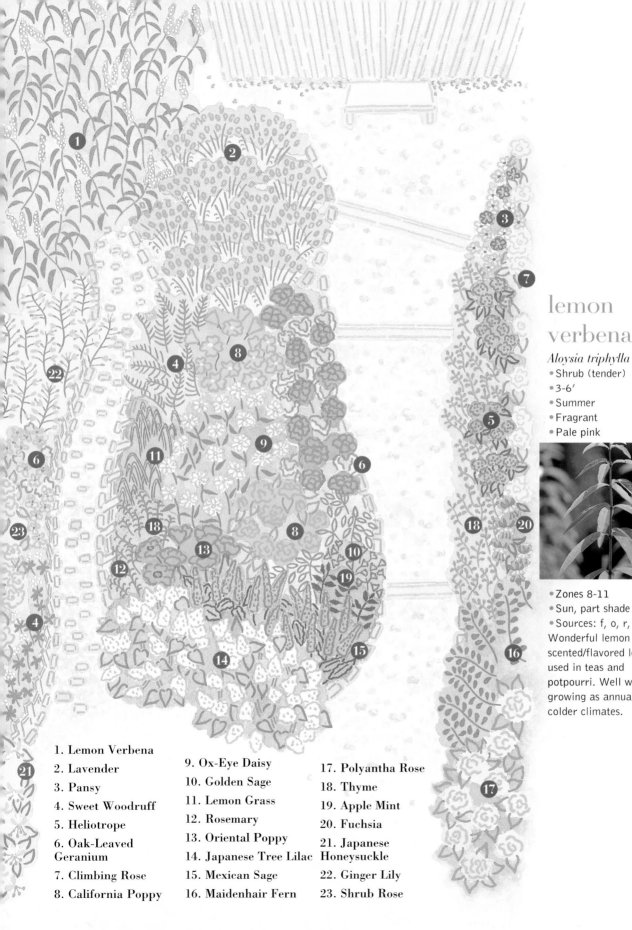

lavender

Lavandula spp.
- Perennial, evergreen herb
- 12-36"
- Early summer
- Fragrant
- Purple/violet
- Zones 5-8
- Sun
- Sources: f, s, v, ff, gg

Use flowers fresh or hang to dry. Cut stems after flowering for rebloom. Prefers well-drained soil.

lemon verbena

Aloysia triphylla
- Shrub (tender)
- 3-6'
- Summer
- Fragrant
- Pale pink

- Zones 8-11
- Sun, part shade
- Sources: f, o, r, v

Wonderful lemon scented/flavored leaves; used in teas and potpourri. Well worth growing as annual in colder climates.

pansy

Viola x *wittrockiana* hyb.
- Annual
- 6-9"
- Spring
- White to purple
- Part shade
- Sources: cc, dd

Start seed indoors 12 weeks before spring frost-free date. Prefers cool weather; moist, organic soil. Fall-planted pansies overwinter in most areas.

1. Lemon Verbena
2. Lavender
3. Pansy
4. Sweet Woodruff
5. Heliotrope
6. Oak-Leaved Geranium
7. Climbing Rose
8. California Poppy
9. Ox-Eye Daisy
10. Golden Sage
11. Lemon Grass
12. Rosemary
13. Oriental Poppy
14. Japanese Tree Lilac
15. Mexican Sage
16. Maidenhair Fern
17. Polyantha Rose
18. Thyme
19. Apple Mint
20. Fuchsia
21. Japanese Honeysuckle
22. Ginger Lily
23. Shrub Rose

sweet woodruff

Galium odoratum
- Perennial, herb
- 6-8″
- Late spring
- White
- Zones 5-10
- Shade, part shade
- Sources: f, aa

Good shade groundcover. Dried leaves have vanilla scent. Use fresh for potpourri and May wine.

oak-leaved geranium

Pelargonium quercifolium
- Annual, herb
- 1-3′
- Summer
- Fragrant
- Pale pink

- Sun, part shade
- Source: f

Balsam-scented leaves good for potpourri. Prefers well-drained soil. Take cuttings in summer and grow on sunny windowsill in winter.

heliotrope

Heliotropium arborescens
- Shrub (tender)
- 2-4′
- Summer
- Fragrant
- Purple
- Zone 10
- Sun
- Sources: j, s, v, ff

Grown as an annual; great for bedding, containers, or border. Start seed early indoors or purchase plants.

climbing rose

Rosa 'Maréchal Niel'
- Shrub
- 12-15′
- Late spring, summer
- Fragrant
- Yellow
- Zones 8-10
- Full sun
- Source: x

A vigorous climber for mild climates. Huge golden blooms; dark coppery-green leaves. Highly perfumed. Provide a warm, sheltered location.

california poppy

Eschscholzia californica
- Annual
- 8-12″
- Summer-frost
- Orange-yellow
- Sun
- Sources: j, z, dd

Provides a bright accent for border. Sow seed outdoors in well-drained soil. Will self-sow and naturalize if not deadheaded.

ox-eye daisy

Leucanthemum vulgare (*Chrysanthemum leucanthemum*)
- Perennial
- 24″
- Early summer
- White

- Zones 3-10
- Sun
- Sources: j, v, z

Common daisy. Easy to grow. Good for naturalized areas and meadows as it will spread and self-sow. Excellent cut flower. Named varieties.

golden sage

Salvia officinalis 'Icterina'
- Perennial herb
- 12-24″
- Foliage plant
- Fragrant
- Zones 4-8
- Sun
- Sources: f, r

Gold-variegated, aromatic leaves. Less vigorous variety of culinary sage. Prefers well-drained soil. Cut back in spring.

lemon grass

Cymbopogon citratus
- Perennial (tender)
- 3-4′
- Foliage plant
- Medium green
- Zones 9-10
- Sun
- Sources: f, n, v, ii

Stiff lemon-scented leaves; used for tea and Asian cuisine. Attractive landscape grass in warm climates; grow as an annual or in a container in cold winter areas.

rosemary

Rosmarinus officinalis
- Shrub (tender)
- 2-6'
- Summer
- Fragrant
- Blue
- Zones 7-10
- Sun
- Sources: e, f, r, v, cc

Grown for its deep green, resinous leaves used in cooking. Prefers well-drained, moist soil. 'Arp' is hardiest variety.

oriental poppy

Papaver orientale
- Perennial
- 3-4'
- Spring
- White to red
- Zones 3-9
- Sun, part shade
- Sources: ff, ii

Wiry stems with 6- to 10-inch, crepe paperlike flowers. Prefers well-drained soil. Self-sows. Goes dormant by midsummer.

japanese tree lilac

Syringa reticulata
- Shrub
- 20-30'
- Late spring, early summer
- Fragrant
- Creamy White

- Zones 3-7
- Sun
- Sources: a, e, g

Good in city street planting as a specimen or in groups. Grow in a tree shape or as a multistemmed shrub. Trouble-free, late blooming lilac.

mexican sage

Salvia leucantha
- Perennial (tender)
- 3-5'
- Late summer to fall
- Purple with white
- Zones 8-11
- Sun, part shade
- Sources: e, f, n, ff, jj

Velvety, purple bracts on arching stems attract hummingbirds in fall. Grow as an annual in cold winter areas. Make cuttings in fall.

maidenhair fern

Adiantum pedatum
- Fern
- 18-36"
- Foliage plant
- Zones 3-8
- Shade, part shade
- Sources: e, g, y, ii

Graceful in woodland or formal gardens. Bright green fronds on black stems. Prefers moist, organic soil.

polyantha rose

Rosa 'Cécile Brünner'
- Shrub
- 30-36"
- Summer, reblooms
- Fragrant
- Light pink

- Zones 6-9
- Sun
- Source: x

The original "sweetheart" rose with perfect buds; small glossy leaves. Upright habit. Not hardy in severe climates. Disease resistant. Requires only light pruning.

thyme

Thymus vulgaris
- Perennial herb
- 6-15"
- Summer
- Fragrant
- White to lilac
- Zones 4-9
- Sun, part shade
- Sources: f, dd

Gray-green, aromatic leaves and flowers used in cooking. Needs well-drained soil; wet soil rots the plant.

apple mint

Mentha suaveolens
- Perennial herb
- 12-36"
- Summer
- Fragrant
- White, pink
- Zones 5-10
- Sun, part shade
- Sources: f, o, v

Attractive leaves with slight apple scent, fruity flavor. To keep mints from spreading, contain in a bottomless nursery pot plunged into the soil, with 1 inch showing above ground.

fuchsia

Fuchsia 'Swingtime'
- Perennial (tender)
- 1-3'
- Summer
- White with red
- Zones 8-11
- Part shade
- Source: ii

Hummingbird magnet. Especially attractive in hanging baskets or trained as a standard. Treat as an annual in cold winter areas. Don't let the soil dry out.

ginger lily

Hedychium gardnerianum
- Perennial (tender)
- 4-6'
- Summer–fall
- Fragrant
- Yellow
- Zones 9-10
- Sun, part shade
- Sources: dd, jj

Perfect plant for that tropical look; lemon yellow flowers with showy, bright red stamens and long shiny leaves. Heady perfume. Can be invasive.

japanese honeysuckle

Lonicera japonica 'Halliana'
- Vine, perennial
- 20' length
- Summer
- Fragrant
- White, fades to buff
- Zones 5-9
- Sun, part shade
- Sources: e, g, gg

Valued ornamental as a groundcover or screen. Nectarous blooms. Aggressive.

shrub rose

Rosa 'Alchymist'
- Shrub
- 8'
- Early summer
- Fragrant
- Apricot
- Zones 5-9
- Sun
- Sources: x, ii

Support on a trellis or pillar. Attractive bronze to dark green leaves. Disease resistant. Perfumed, long-lasting, double flowers.

bright

border

g

ardening is the ultimate living art form. And, the love of beauty and color will guide you in your gardening decisions. You need the patience to learn from experience, the willingness to experiment, and the ability to use nature's entire color palette. Two Denver artists show the way by using tough and durable plants with bright, strong colors.

Turn on the lights with vivid border colors. *Opposite*: 'Irish Eyes' black-eyed Susan.

Living in Denver was a new gardening experience for botanical illustrator Michael Eagleton and his wife, Kate. Like any other gardeners who move to a new location, their first priority was to establish the garden. They wanted to give their overgrown yard a country feeling.

First on the list was increasing the amount of sunlight the garden received. To do this, Michael pruned many of the lower limbs of the deciduous trees growing in their yard, effectively raising the level of the canopy. He gave the shrubs a healthy

pruning as well.

The goal was to have spectacular displays of flowers for as long as possible. This is easier said than done in an area like Denver, with a short growing season and dramatic temperature swings–from 80 degrees one day to snow the next in spring and fall. So Michael and Kate selected plants that would provide color and thrive in this climate.

Sweet autumn clematis is a particularly valuable country garden plant that grows vigorously each season and covers large areas. Michael and Kate grew it on a trellis scaling the side of the house. Its small, white flowers render a sweet scent that

high altitude, bright color garden

wafts a great distance in the garden, especially on late summer nights

Michael and Kate love plants with brilliant colors that paint their garden in broad, bold sweeps. They planted red crocosmias, magenta rose campion, and scarlet Maltese cross. They don't worry much about clashing colors and try to attain a wild, color-filled border that suggests the look of a natural meadow.

From the entry into the garden, stepping stones form a path for a relaxed stroll. Interplanting with prostrate speedwell, mazus, and thyme softens the hard edges of the stones. Plants splash the area with color, perpetuating the country garden look.

The artists' retreat now hosts well over 110 varieties of perennials. The earliest flower of the year is the Christmas rose. Spring follows with snowdrops, pasque-flower, bloodroot, jack-in-the-pulpit, shooting star, wild ginger, and other early bulbs and wildflowers.

In summer, meadow rue, astilbe, turtlehead, monkshood, many lilies, and several shades of monarda take the spotlight. The gardening season closes with late annuals, lilies, sunflower, hardy ageratum, Japanese anemone, and sweet autumn clematis.

TOUGH PLANTS
Many silvery-leafed plants are quite tough, and they're all drought tolerant. Lamb's ears (*Stachys byzantina*) are favorite edging plants. Try the large-leafed *Stachys* 'Helena von Stein' (similar to the less elegantly named, 'Big Ears'). 'Cotton Ball' bears unusually showy, white flowers.

Sea lavenders (*Eryngium* spp.) belie their name. Not at all delicate, they are are striking with their stiffly cupped, fully armed, spiny leaves. Leave them in the garden through winter; their form persists. The pale *E. giganteum* 'Miss Willmott's Ghost' is outstanding in an evening garden. A biennial, it self-sows.

Opposite: Overvi of the garden sho bright flow contrasting with brick hou

A bright, bold entryway garden is always inviting.

Growing plants in the Rocky Mountain region was a new challenge for Mike and Kate Eagleton. So they choose their plants wisely, knowing the growing conditions can be harsh. Each plant is placed carefully, matching its cultural needs with available sunlight, soil, and water conditions. If a plant doesn't do well, the Eagletons move it to a new location. And, if it still doesn't perform, there is the third location in the garden where it must do well, die, or end up on the compost pile. No wimpy plants, please; strength of growth and color dictates how this garden will look.

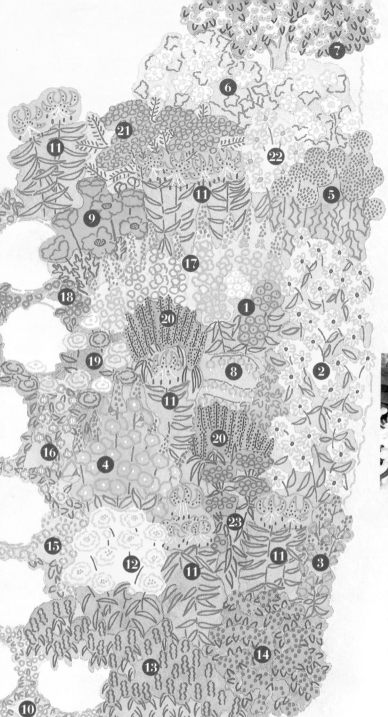

black-eyed susan

Rudbeckia hirta 'Irish Eyes'
- Perennial
- 30-36"
- Summer
- Yellow with green
- Zones 3-10
- Sun
- Sources: s, cc, dd.

Also called 'Green Eyes'; unique flowers good for cutting. Short-lived.

summer phlox

Phlox paniculata
- Perennial
- 2-5'
- Summer-early fall
- Fragrant
- White to red
- Zones 3-9
- Sun
- Sources: i, u, aa

Clump-forming, sweetly scented, old-fashioned, summer flowers. Need good air circulation to avoid mildew. Deadhead to prevent self sowing. Look for named varieties.

penstemon

Penstemon 'Elfin Pink'
- Perennial
- 18"
- Early spring, summer
- Pink
- Zones 3-9
- Sun
- Sources: e, u, ff

Long-blooming hybrid with erect stems over large base of leaves. Perfect drainage a must; add sand and gravel to soil. Don't fertilize.

prairie mallow

Sidalcea malviflora
- Perennial
- 2-4'
- Summer
- Pink to lilac
- Zones 5-10
- Sun, part shade
- Source: ff

Also known as checkerbloom. Many small flowers held above foliage. Prefers sun, but will perform decently in a moist, shady spot.

1. Summer Phlox
2. Black-Eyed Susan
3. Penstemon
4. Prairie Mallow
5. Globe Thistle
6. Thimbleberry
7. Purple-leaf Plum
8. Bleeding Heart
9. Oriental Poppy
10. Lemon Thyme
11. Tiger Lily
12. Tickseed
13. Speedwell
14. Cranberry Cotoneaster
15. Prostrate Speedwell
16. Mazus
17. Obedient Plant
18. Forget-Me-Not
19. English Daisy
20. Salvia
21. Yarrow
22. Saw-Toothed Sunflower
23. Maltese Cross

globe thistle

Echinops ritro
- Perennial
- 2-3'
- Summer
- Blue
- Zones 3-10
- Sun
- Sources: e, ii, jj

White-woolly stems and leaf reverses. Some name confusion. Prickly, round flower heads. Use flowers freshly cut or dried.

thimbleberry

Rubus parviflorus
- Shrub
- 6'
- Summer
- Red fruit
- Zones 3-8
- Sun
- Source: e

Edible raspberrylike fruit used in preserves and jellies. Somewhat ornamental plant. Likes moist, organic soils.

purple-leaf plum

Prunus cerasifera 'Thundercloud'
- Tree
- 15-30'
- Early spring
- Fragrant
- Pink

- Zones 5-8
- Sun
- Sources: e, g

Lightly scented flowers appear before tree leafs out; deep purple foliage holds all season. Prune after flowers fade. May have a shrubby form. Prefers well-drained soil.

bleeding heart

Dicentra spectabilis
- Perennial
- 2-3'
- Spring-summer
- Pink
- Zones 3-10
- Part shade
- Sources: g, aa, ii

Old favorite with ferny foliage. Arching stems; delicate flowers. Dies back in midsummer.

oriental poppy

Papaver orientale
- Perennial
- 3-4'
- Spring
- Red to white
- Zones 3-9
- Sun, part shade
- Sources: ff, ii

Big, crinkled, crepe-paperlike, 6-inch diameter flowers sway on wiry stems. Does not like to be moved; long taproot. Goes dormant by midsummer.

lemon thyme

Thymus 'Minus'
- Perennial, herb
- 1"
- Summer, early fall
- Fragrant
- Lavender
- Zones 4-8
- Sun
- Sources: g, bb, ff

Tiniest thyme; good carpet plant or between paving stones. Needs perfect drainage. Aromatic leaves.

tiger lily

Lilium lancifolium (*L. tigrinum*)
- Bulb
- 3-4'
- Late summer
- Orange with black spots
- Zones 3-9
- Sun
- Source: ii

Easy garden favorite. Don't plant near other lilies, as it carries a virus. Needs well-drained, rich soil.

tickseed

Coreopsis grandiflora
'Sunray'
- Perennial
- 18-30"
- Summer
- Vivid gold
- Zones 5-10
- Sun
- Sources: e, gg

Somewhat hairy plant; double flowers. Easy to grow in decent soil. Propagate by cuttings.

speedwell

Veronica austriaca
'Crater Lake Blue'
- Perennial
- 12"
- Spring
- Blue
- Zones 6-8
- Sun
- Sources: e, dd, ii

One of the best of all the veronicas with many blue flowers. Support lightly, using twigs or brush. Cut back after flowering.

cranberry cotoneaster

Cotoneaster apiculatus
- Shrub
- 3', spread to 6'
- Late spring
- Pink
- Zones 4-7

- Sun, part shade
- Sources: e, g, ff, gg

Low, spreading shrub; can be used as a groundcover for erosion control or as a foundation plant. Stems form interesting herringbone pattern. Vibrant red berries in fall persist into winter. Prefers moist, well-drained soil.

prostrate speedwell

Veronica prostrata
'Mrs. Holt'
- Perennial
- 3-6", spread to 18"
- Summer
- Bluish pink
- Zones 4-8
- Sun
- Sources: e, y

Creeping form of speedwell. Easy to grow in sunny, well-drained spot.

mazus

Mazus reptans
- Perennial
- 1-3"
- Late spring
- Violet
- Zones 3-9
- Shade, part shade
- Sources: o, n, y, ff, gg

Dense, prostrate groundcover. Quickly spreads in shady areas. Plant between stepping stones.

obedient plant

Physotegia virginiana
- Perennial
- 3-5'
- Summer-fall
- Red-violet to white
- Zones 3-10
- Sun, part shade
- Sources: u, gg, ii

Clump-forming plant is well suited to borders or wildflower gardens. Good cutting flower; long blooming. Easy to grow; divide every 2 to 3 years to rejuvenate the plant and keep it within bounds.

forget-me-not

Myosotis sylvatica
- Biennial
- 9-24"
- White to purple
- Zones 5-9
- Part shade
- Sources: y, cc, dd

Once established, it will self-sow each year. Or, grow as an annual; sow seed indoors in March.

english daisy

Bellis perennis
- Perennial
- 6-8"
- Late spring, early summer
- White to red
- Zones 3-10
- Sun, part shade
- Sources: s, dd

Wonderful as edging or as cover for spring-blooming bulbs. Various colors; singles and semidouble flowers available.

salvia

Salvia 'Blue Queen'
- Perennial
- 12-18"
- Summer, fall
- Blue
- Zones 5-10
- Sun
- Sources: b, e, dd

Hybrid; forms nice dwarf clump. Numerous flowers; cut off spent flowers for reblooming. Grows best in well-drained, organic soil. Fertilize in growing season.

saw-toothed sunflower

Helianthus grosse-serratus
- Perennial
- 12-15'
- Fall
- Bright yellow
- Zones 4-10
- Source: q

Big, perennial sunflower; woody stems at base. Robust plants for naturalizing or back of border.

yarrow

Achillea 'Apple Blossom' ('Apfelblute')
- Perennial
- 2-3'
- Summer
- Pink, rose
- Zones 2-10
- Sun
- Sources: e, ff

Flat clusters of flowers; feathery foliage. Great for bouquets—fresh or dried. Grows well in sunny spot in well-drained soil.

maltese cross

Lychnis chalcedonica
- Perennial
- 3-5'
- Summer
- Bright scarlet
- Zones 3-10
- Sun
- Sources: e, t, hh

Intense red-scarlet flowers in dense clusters. Plant behind other plants; may need staking. Requires very well-drained soil.

vertical accents

Structure and layout define the success of this New England garden. Clean, geometric forms are delineated by stone walls, paths, gates, a pavilion, and trellises. Vertical accents create height; you can look up and see climbing clematis and catch the scent of roses. Together, these elements form the backbone of the garden—the hardscape that controls the lush plantings bursting forth in gentle chaos.

frederick Rice fell in love with the chaos of naturalistic, loose plantings contained within a series of garden rooms–the gardening philosophy espoused by the early 20th-century English garden designer Gertrude Jekyll. This look requires strong structure—the bones of the garden—including walls, paths, and fences.

In New England and other cold-weather areas, the bones of the garden take on added importance because they're exposed in winter. Taking this into consideration, Frederick built a semicircular brick path, long flowing borders, and stone walls. Together these improvements gave depth to the relatively modest 101 × 120-foot property.

After setting the structures, Frederick began the garden. He wanted the plantings to have the freedom to grow, sway, or tumble naturally, creating the feeling of a relaxed and picturesque Victorian cottage garden. Vining plants, trained upwards, vertically accent the garden. The wild abandon of colors and textures makes the perfect foil for the angular structures. 'Harison's Yellow' climbing rose, the earliest to bloom in the garden, abundantly covers the rustic entrance gate. A strong trellis tames the trumpet vine, an aggressive climber and hummingbird magnet.

The paths meander through the garden, one threading its way through a trellised arbor into an herb garden. Clematis 'Ville de Lyon', with its large purple and white flowers scales the side of the trellis on the way to the vegetable garden. Another path leads up a flight of granite steps overlooking the whole garden.

Well-used old bricks, chipped, irregularly shaped and colored, or stones, interplanted and slightly overrun with tiny groundcovers, make appropriate footpaths to Frederick's wooden pavilion, ideal for breakfast or afternoon tea. Climbing roses wrap around it while densely planted hollyhocks, lamb's ears, potentillas, and columbines surround the base. These vertical flourishes cap the garden like exclamation points— excited to announce the incomparable beauty of their surroundings.

accenting the bones of a garden

GLORIOUS CLIMBERS
The genus *Ipomoea* includes many terrific annual vines. Annuals have one great advantage: If for any reason they fail to please one year, don't plant them the next.

Morning glories (*Ipomoea tricolor*) twine their way skyward, opening in the early morning and closing by afternoon. Pair them with their night-blooming cousins, moonflowers (*I. alba*), for iridescent white flowers that open at sunset, perfuming the summer night air.

'Blackie' sweet potato (*I. batatas*), a very popular vine, will produce large, edible tubers. But it's grown mainly for its deep burgundy, trilobed leaves. Pair it with chartreuse-leafed 'Marguerite' for impact.

Use containers of plants to draw your eye away from areas in the garden that are past bloom. *Opposite:* Overview of garden.

Vertical accents act as bold exclamation points

in a Victorian-style cottage garden. Floral designer Frederick Rice's horticultural roots run deep in the New England soil surrounding the home his grandfather built in 1927. Yet, his aesthetic training was honed in the historic gardens of England. Immediately upon his return from England, Frederick began to apply renowned landscape designer Gertrude Jekyll's philosophy to his family home, creating a lush garden with strong structures and overflowing gardens. By letting the land speak to him, Frederick created a vision that would have year-round impact.

fern-leaf peony

Paeonia tenuifolia
'Plena'
- Perennial
- 12-30"
- Spring
- Fragrant
- Red

- Zones 4-10
- Sun, part shade
- Sources: e, l

Elegant fern-leaf foliage lasts long after double flowers fade. Takes 2 to 3 years to establish, and worth the wait. Brittle rhizome. Plant dies down midsummer.

coralbells

Heuchera americana
'Ruby Veil'
- Perennial
- 12"
- Late spring, early summer
- White
- Zones 4-9
- Part shade
- Sources: i, u

Ruby-red leaves touched with slate gray add sparkle at ground level. Tolerate more sun if in moist, well-drained soil.

johnny-jump-up

Viola tricolor
- Annual
- 12"
- Early spring
- Purple with yellow
- Sun, part shade
- Sources: t, v, dd

Favorite for interplanting among daffodils and tulips in spring. Self-sows; a garden can't have too many of these cheerful blooms. Edible flowers. Thrives in cool weather.

variegated iris

Iris pallida
'Aurea Variegata'
- Perennial
- 3-4'
- Late spring
- Fragrant
- Soft lilac blue

- Zones 3-10
- Sun
- Sources: e, ii

Also known as orris root. Handsomely striped foliage most of the year, which makes a nice accent even without flowers. Sweetly scented blooms.

comfrey

Symphytum officinale
- Perennial, herb
- 3-5'
- Spring to frost
- White to red
- Zones 3-10
- Sun, part shade
- Sources: f, o

Easy, fast-growing, background plant. Can be invasive; contain in a nursery pot.

trumpet vine

Campsis radicans
- Vine, perennial
- Length to 40'
- Summer
- Orange to red
- Zones 4-9
- Sun, part shade
- Sources: a, y, dd

Attracts hummingbirds. Aggressive vine; sends out suckers. Prune to keep in bounds. Blooms on new wood. Less aggressive when grown in poor, dry soil.

rhododendron

Rhododendron 'Scintillation'
- Shrub, evergreen
- 6'
- Early spring
- Fragrant
- Pink, amber throat
- Zones 5-9
- Sun, part shade
- Sources: g, y

One of the best rhododendrons; good substance and form. Dark green, lustrous leaves. Heat tolerant. Mulch in late spring to keep roots cool.

french tarragon

Artemisia dracunculus
- Perennial, herb
- 2'
- No flowers
- Fragrant foliage
- Zones 3- 9
- Sun, part shade
- Sources: e, f, o, v

Culinary herb. Must be propagated from cuttings; or buy plants. Needs well-drained, organic soil.

thyme

Thymus spp.
- Perennial, herb
- 12"
- Summer
- Fragrant
- Pink to purple
- Zones 5-9
- Sun
- Sources: e, u, y

Many varieties, some with variegated leaves. Most for culinary use. Shear back in early spring. Must have good drainage, or it will rot.

leadwort

Plumbago auriculata 'Monott'
- Perennial (tender)
- 4-6'
- Summer to fall
- Pale blue
- Zones 9-10
- Sun
- Sources: n, o

Tropical plant grown as an annual. Covered with many light blue flowers. In cold winter climates, take cuttings in fall to overwinter.

clematis

Clematis 'Ville de Lyon'
- Vine, perennial
- 8-14'
- Late spring-fall
- Deep carmine
- Zones 4-9
- Sun
- Sources: e, f, ii

Very vigorous; needs support. Plant so roots are in shade, leaves and flowers in sun. Prefers well-drained, organic soil; mulch. Try growing it up an evergreen.

bee balm

Monarda 'Marshall's Delight'
- Perennial
- 3-4'
- Early summer
- Fragrant
- Pink
- Zones 4-9
- Sun, part shade
- Sources: e, f, q, v, ii

Large flowers attract hummingbirds. Aromatic leaves. Mildew resistant. Prefers moist soil; needs good air circulation. Spreads quickly.

southernwood

Artemisia abrotanum 'Lemon Scented'
- Perennial, herb
- 3-5'
- Summer
- Yellow
- Zones 4-8
- Sun
- Sources: n, o, q, v

Ornamental with aromatic, feathery, gray-green leaves. Easy to grow in well-drained soil. Good foil or backdrop for hot colors.

common moss rose

Rosa x *centifolia muscosa*
- Shrub
- 4-6'
- Late spring, early summer
- Pink
- Fragrant
- Zones 4-9
- Sun
- Source: x

Very fragrant; blooms only once. Curious mosslike "whiskers" on unopened buds.

chives

Allium schoenoprasum
- Perennial, herb
- 18"
- Early summer
- Blue-purple
- Zones 3-10
- Sun
- Sources: j, t, hh

Easy to grow. Ornamental and edible leaves and month-long flowers. Shear after flowering.

calendula

Calendula officinalis
- Annual, herb
- 18"
- Summer to fall
- Yellow to orange
- Sun
- Sources: e, v, dd

Also known as pot marigold. Useful herb for dyes, cosmetics, and culinary uses (edible flowers). Many attractive varieties available. Grows in average soil; self-sows.

cranesbill

Geranium incanum
- Perennial, tender
- 6-8"
- Spring to fall
- Pink, magenta
- Zones 5-10

- Sun
- Sources: buy locally

Bushy mounds of delicate, divided leaves; deep pink flowers. Trim after flowering to encourage rebloom. Prefers a warm, sunny spot.

lungwort

Pulmonaria 'Spilled Milk'
- Perennial
- 9"
- Spring
- Rose to blue
- Zones 3-9
- Shade, part shade
- Source: e

Early flowering, bright accent for shade. Shear plants after first bloom for added vigor and better shape. Grows well in moist soil.

corydalis

Corydalis lutea
- Perennial
- 12-15"
- Spring to fall
- Yellow
- Zones 5-10
- Sun, shade
- Sources: s, dd, ii

Durable; will grow in walls and between stepping stones. Long blooming with fernlike foliage. Mounding form.

climbing rose

Rosa 'American Pillar'
- Shrub
- 15-20'
- Summer to fall
- Bright pink, white eye

- Zones: 5-9
- Sun
- Source: x

Vigorous, upright grower. Huge clusters of 2- to 3-inch flowers with no fragrance. Decorative red hips in late fall attract birds.

golden oregano

Origanum vulgare 'Aureum'
- Perennial, herb
- 1-2'
- Summer to fall
- Rose-lilac, lavender
- Zones 5-9
- Sun
- Sources: o, v, y

Useful ornamental with golden, aromatic leaves. Requires well-drained soil and full sun.

sweet cicely

Myrrhis odorata
- Perennial, herb
- 3'
- Late spring, early summer
- Fragrant
- White
- Zones 3-10
- Part shade, sun
- Sources: o, v

Sweetly scented, fern-like foliage. Spreads, yet controllable. Roots and leaves used in cooking.

feverfew

Tanacetum parthenium
- Perennial, herb
- 2-3′
- Midsummer to fall
- Fragrant
- White with yellow
- Zones 4-9
- Sun, part shade
- Sources: f, r, v

Lots of small daisylike flowers; scented leaves. Dry flowers for arrangements. Easy to grow in average soil.

zinnia

Zinnia elegans hyb.
- Annual
- 24-36″
- Summer
- White to red
- Sun
- Source: b

Easy to grow. Bright flowers for cutting. Start seed indoors 4 weeks before last frost or direct seed outdoors. Likes warmth.

spiderwort

Tradescantia virginiana hyb.
- Perennial
- 18-36″
- Late spring to fall
- White to blue
- Zones 4-10
- Sun, shade
- Sources: u, aa

Native plant that will grow almost anywhere; best in part shade. Long blooming season. Many nice new hybrids.

grape

Vitis vinifera
- Vine, woody
- 6-10′
- Fall fruit
- Zones 5-10
- Sun
- Sources: b, p

Ornamental vine; special pruning needed for fruit. Requires well-drained, deep, rich, organic soil, and good air circulation.

dappled

shade

garden

despite the appeal of a sunny garden, many gardeners find themselves with varying amounts of shade, especially as trees grow taller and mature. Dappled shade, with its shimmering light, is especially attractive to gardeners in regions with hot summers. In dappled shade, they can grow many sun-loving plants as well as a wide array of plants that thrive in a greater degree of shade.

Airy columbines allow you to see beyond the front of the border. *Opposite: Veronica 'Red Fox'.*

for many gardeners, planting a dappled shade garden involves some trial and error until they learn the exact intensities of light. Shade also affects air

and soil temperature. It's cooler in the shade, often as much as 15 degrees, making shade especially appealing in hot summer areas.

When choosing plants for this type of garden, consider the leaf textures rather than trying to achieve a single season of blooming color.

Foliage is the key element of design—look to the leaves' textures, shapes, and various hues of green to provide multiseason interest. Combinations such as a pale green, filigreed fern planted next to the solid,

yet undulating, gray-green leaves of lady's mantle provide much visual interest. The added bonus: In late spring, the lady's mantle sends up its chartreuse flower sprays.

Hostas, with their bold leaves, are the workhorses of shade gardens. Over the years, hybridizers have created a vast array of leaf

shapes, colors, and sizes for diversity. Hostas are versatile: They create a framework for most plantings, edge a bed or border, or produce a color accent with leaves of blue-green through gold. Variegated varieties are especially preferred for brightening a dark corner. The flowers of some hostas add a fragrant note to the summer garden. Many have white flowers which

stand out in the shade. Hosta leaves also camouflage fading foliage of short-season perennials or bulbs. Plant them among the hostas so they will grow through the leaves.

Shade gardens need not be devoid of color or flowers. There are many more flowering plants for dappled or partial shade than you might think. Some favorites are epimedium (white, red, or yellow flowers), astilbe (white, pink, or red), hellebores (white,

pink, green, or purple), meadow rue (yellow or pink), and yellow celandine poppies.

Variegated leaves also provide color. Experiment with variegated hostas, Japanese painted fern, and lungworts.

Although you can't

plant a formal rose garden in shade, you can use some sun-loving plants in dappled shade. Look for bright spots—where the sun shines clearly for several hours each day. Reserve these areas for sun-loving favorites you just can't live without.

KNOW YOUR SHADE

Various types of shade have different light levels, which dictate what will grow.

Dappled Shade: A pattern of light (no direct sun) moving across the ground, created by open trees. It provides the most light, giving the widest range of plant possibilities.

Open Shade: Bright light, but no direct sun, from a northern exposure with walls or buildings casting shadows.

Part Shade: An area that receives direct sun part of the day and shade the remainder of the day. Morning light is less scorching to most plants than afternoon.

Deep or Dense Shade: The deepest shade is found in north-facing yards or where tall walls or fences block most of the light except for tiny strips.

creating your **shade** garden

To create an intimate garden next to the house,

Mary Reedy abandoned her old design style, which called for large, bold drifts of plants. In this St. Louis, Missouri, garden, she concentrated on color harmonies and created an intimate garden right outside her door, so she can throw open a window and smell the lilies and see the beauty.

It's a highly personal space for her must-have plants (peonies and daylilies). Mary is an avid plant collector, so she allowed room for planting single specimens (a no-no under previous rules). There is always space to plant one more treasure and give it time to mature.

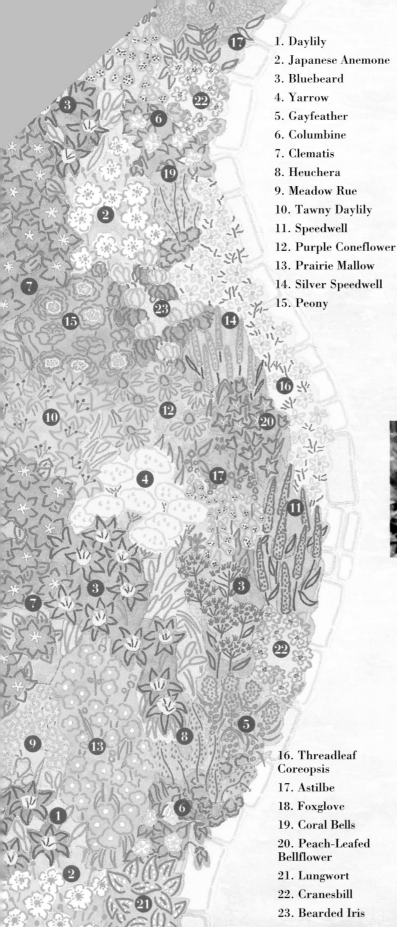

japanese anemone

Anemone x *hybrida*
- Perennial
- 3-4'
- Late summer-early fall
- White to deep pink
- Zones 5-10
- Part shade, sun
- Sources: s, hh, ii

Valuable plant; elegant 2- to 3-inch flowers. Prefers moist soil.

daylily

Hemerocallis 'Malachie'
- Perennial
- 2-4'
- Summer-fall
- Rose, yellow throat
- Zones 4-10
- Sun, part shade
- Source: ee

A solid performer. Prefers full sun and moist, rich soil, but is forgiving of adverse conditions. Divide every 3 years. Interplant with daffodils or tulips.

yarrow

Achillea 'Coronation Gold'
- Perennial
- 3'
- Summer
- Yellow

- Zones 3-10
- Sun
- Source: ii

Indispensable in summer gardens; elegant ferny foliage adds texture. Good for cutting and drying. Prefers well-drained soil. Drought tolerant.

bluebeard

Caryopteris x *clandonensis* 'Blue Mist'
- Shrub
- 3'
- Summer
- Blue
- Zones 7-10
- Part shade, sun
- Sources: a, i

Grow it like a perennial; cut it down to several inches above ground in early spring. Prefers well-drained soil.

gayfeather

Liatris spicata 'Kobold'
- Perennial
- 1.5-3'
- Summer to fall
- Zones 3-10
- Purple-violet
- Sun
- Sources: e, j, s, ff, ii

Prefers somewhat fertile soil without winter wetness.

columbine

Aquilegia caerulea 'Crimson Star'
- Perennial
- 24"
- Summer
- Various
- Zones 3-10
- Part shade, sun
- Source: j

Elegantly divided leaves. Thrives and bloom for months in soils with good drainage. Long-spurred, bicolor flowers.

clematis

Clematis x *jackmanii*
- Vine, perennial
- Up to 12'
- Summer to fall
- Zones 3-9
- Sun, part shade
- Sources: b, e, gg

Prefers its roots in shady, fertile, moist soil

and its leaves and flowers in sun. Mulch well to keep roots cool. An elegant favorite with large flowers. Plant to twine with climbing roses.

heuchera

Heuchera 'Chocolate Ruffles'
- Perennial
- 12-24"
- Late spring, early summer
- White
- Zones 4-9
- Part shade
- Sources: u, y

Superb foliage plant; long-lived, ruffled, deep chocolate-brown leaves, purple underneath. Prefers moist soil.

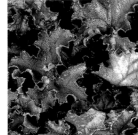

meadow rue

Thalictrum rochebrunianum
- Perennial
- 4-6'
- Summer-early fall
- Purple/pink to lavender
- Zones 5-10
- Part shade, sun
- Sources: i, aa, ii

Delicate leaves; graceful flopping habit. Easy to grow anywhere. Likes moist, organic soil.

tawny daylily

Hemerocallis fulva
- Perennial
- 24-30"
- Summer
- Orange-red

- Zones 4-10
- Sun, part shade
- Source: ee

Easy to grow. Edible flowers. Naturalizes well; best suited for wild areas. Excellent plant for erosion control. Prefers average soil. Named varieties available.

speedwell

Veronica 'Blue Charm'
- Perennial
- 12"
- Summer
- Lavender blue
- Zones 3-10
- Part shade, sun
- Source: y

Covered with many spikes of lavender-blue flowers. Easy to grow in average, well-drained soil. Great cut flower.

purple coneflower

Echinacea purpurea
- Perennial
- 3-4'
- Summer
- Purple
- Zones 3-10
- Sun
- Sources: q, dd, jj

Easy-to-grow North American native. Handsome 3-inch, daisylike flowers. Prefers a sunny, well-drained spot.

silver speedwell

Veronica incana 'Red Fox'
- Perennial
- 12"
- Summer
- Deep rose
- Zones 3-10
- Sun, part shade
- Sources: e, y

Easy to grow in well-drained, average soil.

astilbe

Astilbe chinensis 'Fanal'
- Perennial
- 18"
- Summer
- Pink
- Zones 4-8
- Part shade, sun
- Sources: c, y

Nicely compact variety. Good performer with a long blooming season. Prefers moist, well-drained soil.

prairie mallow

Sidalcea malviflora 'Party Girl'
- Perennial
- 2-4'
- Summer

- Pink
- Zones 5-10
- Sun to part shade
- Source: ff

Also known as checkerbloom and false mallow. Attractive perennial with many small flowers held above the foliage. Prefers sun, but will perform decently in a moist, shady spot.

threadleaf coreopsis

Coreopsis verticillata 'Moonbeam'
- Perennial
- 2'
- Summer to fall
- Yellow

- Zones 3-10
- Sun
- Sources: e, g, q, y, ii

Attractive, delicate, erect foliage. Long season; numerous pale yellow flowers. Very drought tolerant.

coral bells

Heuchera 'Susanna'
- Perennial
- 20"
- Spring to summer
- Pink
- Zones 3-10
- Part shade, sun

- Sources: i, u, aa

Long season; fine performer. Grows best in organic soil with good drainage. Many new decorative leaved varieties available.

peony

Paeonia lactiflora hyb.
- Late spring, early summer
- 2-4'
- Summer
- Fragrant
- White to red
- Zones 2-10
- Sun
- Sources: l, gg

Old garden favorite; magnificent 3- to 4-inch, many-petaled, richly perfumed flowers. Requires deep, rich, organic soil and full sun.

foxglove

Digitalis purpurea
- Biennial
- 2-3'
- Late spring to summer
- White to purple
- Zones 3-10
- Part shade, sun
- Sources: t, z, dd

Upright flowering spikes of many bell-shaped flowers. Self-sows, so it seems perennial. Deadhead for second flush of bloom. Poisonous plant.

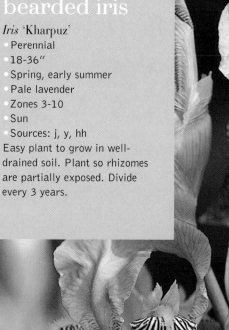

peach-leafed bellflower

Campanula persicifolia
- Perennial
- 2-3′
- Summer
- Blue
- Zones 3-10
- Part shade, sun
- Sources: e, y, z

Prefers moist soil. Large-flowered, white, and double forms. A classic country bloom.

cranesbill

Geranium cinereum 'Ballerina'
- Perennial
- 1′
- Late spring to summer
- Violet-pink
- Zones 4-10
- Sun, part shade
- Sources: e, y, ff, ii

True geranium. Vigorous; good bloomer throughout summer. Plant at the base of tall perennials.

lungwort

Pulmonaria saccharata 'Roy Davidson'
- Perennial
- 8-18″
- Spring
- Pink, turning blue
- Zones 3-9
- Shade
- Sources: u, y, ff

Long-season interest; shiny, long, narrow leaves with silver-gray spots. Easy to grow; prefers moist soil.

bearded iris

Iris 'Kharpuz'
- Perennial
- 18-36″
- Spring, early summer
- Pale lavender
- Zones 3-10
- Sun
- Sources: j, y, hh

Easy plant to grow in well-drained soil. Plant so rhizomes are partially exposed. Divide every 3 years.

sunny

border

beneath Georgia pines, a garden of fond memories

and childhood scents emerges under the high canopy.

Ann Snuggs surrounds herself with the same

flowers that perfumed the air in her great aunt's

garden—gardenia, tuberose,

sweet olive, pinks, Confederate

jasmine, sweet William, and

lily-of-the-valley. The pines

give the illusion of shade,

although the garden is sunny.

'New Dawn' rose trained on a dark trellis gives a cool look in a warm climate. *Opposite*: Tuberose.

color glows under a pine canopy

in this southern garden, Ann and Joe Snuggs enjoy their "blue walk" of hydrangeas that turn a deep periwinkle in the acid soil under the dappled shade of pines. The garden curves, shade turns to sun, and perennials abound. The couple's old-fashioned country favorites include lamb's ears, gooseneck loosestrife, sedum, coneflower, yarrow, hollyhock, bee balm, and daylilies.

Actually, this garden is a collaborative effort. Ann envisioned perennials, while Joe preferred the shade. The towering pines sway and whisper with the wind that is now scented with the flowers of Ann's childhood.

Flanked by crape myrtles, a wide walkway leads through an opening in the garden. A lattice-covered gazebo offers shelter. An arbor covered with 'New Dawn' roses frames a second approach to a grass path which leads into the "secret garden." It's not visible from the lawn, but is awash in a flood of green and white, blooming from early spring through summer with G.G. Gurbling azaleas, wild strawberries, white violets, white impatiens, spirea, oak leaf hydrangeas, hostas, and ferns in a succession of color. Another arbor in the landscape is covered with silver lace vine near creamy gardenias, all backed by a "wall" of dogwoods.

Scents from plants like these create sweet reminiscence. Scientists agree that, of the five senses, smell is most closely linked to memory.

Scented plants also are relatively pest-free and are avoided by both large and small animals. Sweetheart roses, peppermint geranium, lavender, and camellias perform well in this climate and fill the air with their fragrance. Wandering through the gardens rustling with these scented beauties is pure pleasure.

Aromatic plants also enhance the herb garden. No one can resist the signature aromas of lemon balm, mint, and rosemary.

This garden flowers nearly year-round. Appreciated for their culinary as well as aromatic characteristics, dianthus blooms early in the year and daylilies continue in summer. Until the finale of camellias in November, there's always a flower to smell in the garden—a scent to make a memory.

The sun filters through the canopy, shining on the garden and rewarding the Snuggs with warmth, healthy plants, and more memories in the making.

Passalong Plants

In the South, the tradition of passalong plants is deeply rooted; many gardeners have plants that go back several generations. It's rare to visit someone's garden and admire a plant without being given a "start" for your own garden. And, it's considered poor form just to say thank you; the thanks is expressed when you pass along a piece of your garden.

Passalongs from friends and family played a significant role in this garden's development. A neighbor rooted the roses growing over one trellis. The fragrant gardenia in the secret garden came from a favorite uncle.

Gardening often seems to start as a solitary effort, but soon encompasses a larger communal sharing of plants and information.

The complementary colors of daylilies and hydrangeas evoke a sense of coolness. *Opposite:* Garden overview.

The high-limbed, *rustling pines* create their own

garden music. The pines seem cool, yet the branches are high enough that this Atlanta, Georgia, garden remains quite sunny, but relieved of the glaring heat of midday. Under the tall pines, a year-round country garden unfolds. A hydrangea-lined walk leads to tiny violets tucked between paving stones. Though Ann Snuggs gardens on half an acre, she is drawn to details everywhere—tiny vignettes of sylvan beauty, from vine-covered arbors to garden ornaments. In this small space, Ann and her husband take in a world of sights, sounds, and scents.

pinks

Dianthus 'Zing Rose'
- Perennial
- 6-12"
- Summer
- Fragrant
- Rose
- Zones 4-10
- Sun
- Sources: b, s, ii

Clove-scented, 1-inch flowers all summer. Needs well-drained soil.

lemon thyme

Thymus x citriodorus
- Perennial, herb
- 12"
- Summer
- Fragrant
- Pink, pale lilac
- Zones 5-9
- Sun
- Sources: f, r, v

Strongly lemon scented. Keep dry and in sun for optimum flavor; requires well-drained soil. Shear plant in early spring.

black-eyed susan

Rudbeckia hirta hyb.
- Perennial, biennial
- 2-3'
- Summer
- Orange-yellow with black centers

- Zones 4-10
- Sun
- Source: s

Flowers are long lasting; flamboyant color. Many named varieties. Divide every few years.

coneflower

Echinacea purpurea 'White Swan'
- Perennial
- 18-24"
- Summer
- White
- Zones 3-10
- Sun
- Sources: e, gg, ii

Easy, white-flowered, compact selection of North American native. Prefers sunny, well-drained spot.

gardenia

Gardenia augusta (G. jasminoides)
- Shrub, tender
- 4-6'
- Spring
- Fragrant
- White
- Zones 8-10
- Sun
- Sources: n, o

Strongly perfumed, gorgeous, 3-inch, white flowers. Worth growing in pot in colder areas (cool-growing houseplant).

climbing rose

Rosa 'New Dawn'
- Shrub
- 12-15'
- Spring to fall
- Fragrant
- Pink

- Zones 5-9
- Sun
- Sources: x, ii

Everblooming rose that puts on a great show. Fragrant, 3-inch, semidouble flowers. Does well in less than perfect conditions.

hydrangea

Hydrangea macrophylla 'Nikko Blue'
- Shrub
- 6'
- Summer
- Pink/blue, blue/pink
- Zones 6-9
- Sun, part shade
- Sources: a, e, n, gg

Big, "mop-head" flowers. Tough plant. Grow in acid soil for deep-blue flowers.

sweet william

Dianthus barbatus
- Biennial (tender perenn
- 1-2'
- Spring
- Fragrant
- White to purple
- Zones 4-10
- Sun, part shade
- Sources: t, v, z

Blooms second year from seed; may survive in warmer spots. Wide range of color choices.

red valerian

Centranthus ruber
- Perennial
- 18-36″
- Summer
- Fragrant
- Carmine, rose-pink
- Zones 4-10
- Sun, part shade
- Sources: e, v, ii

Lots of tiny, scented flowers; gray-green leaves. Great cut flower. Self-sows.

peppermint geranium

Pelargonium tomentosum
- Perennial, tender
- 18-24″
- Summer
- Fragrant
- Pink

- Zones 9-10
- Sun
- Sources: f, o, v

Aromatic, gray-green leaves. Treat as an annual in cold winter areas; take cuttings or grow as houseplants indoors in winter.

siberian iris

Iris sibirica
- Perennial
- 24-48″
- Late spring, early summer
- White to purple
- Zones 4-10
- Sun, part shade
- Sources: j, ee

Elegant, upright foliage. Tough plant with beautiful flowers. Easy to grow; prefers well-drained, organic soil.

1. Pinks
2. Lemon Thyme
3. Black-Eyed Susan
4. Coneflower
5. Gardenia
6. Climbing Rose
7. Hydrangea
8. Sweet William
9. Peppermint Geranium
10. Red Valerian
11. Siberian Iris
12. Gooseneck Loosestrife
13. Yarrow
14. Tuberose
15. Pansy
16. Daylily
17. Ageratum
18. Lamb's Ears
19. Showy Stonecrop
20. Martagon Lily
21. Salvia
22. Korean Spice Viburnum

yarrow

Achillea filipendulina
- Perennial
- 3-4'
- Summer
- Yellow
- Sun
- Zones 3-10
- Sources: r, y, dd

Elegant fernlike foliage makes a great textural accent. Easy to grow in well-drained soil. Flowers dry well.

gooseneck loosestrife

Lysimachia clethroides
- Perennial
- 30-36"
- Late summer
- White
- Zones 3-10

- Sun, part shade
- Sources: q, y, ii

Elegant upright plant with arching flowers. Can be invasive in good soil; plant in nursery pot and plunge into ground to keep from spreading.

tuberose

Polianthes tuberosa
- Bulb, tender
- 3-4'
- Summer to fall
- Fragrant
- White
- Zones 8-10
- Sun
- Sources: b, n, s, gg

Sweetly perfumed. Good flower for cutting garden, borders, or containers. Easy to grow in rich soil. In zones 7 and colder, dig and store bulbs for the winter.

pansy

Viola x wittrockiana hyb.
- Annual
- 6-9"
- Spring
- Most colors and bicolors
- Part shade
- Sources: cc, dd

Start seed 12 weeks before last frost date. Or, plant in fall for autumn bloom and spring rebloom. Edible flowers. Prefers cool weather; moist, rich soil.

daylily

Hemerocallis 'Goddess'
- Perennial
- 18"
- Summer
- Cream with pink
- Zones 4-9
- Sun
- Source: ee

Small plant, large, 6- to 7-inch flowers. Edible flower. Durable performer in any garden. Divide every few years.

ageratum

Ageratum houstonianum 'Blue Danube'
- Annual
- 6-8", spread to 10"
- Summer
- Sun, part shade
- Sources: b, dd

Abundant clusters of fuzzy flowers. Good in borders or containers. Grows in average soil. Start seed early indoors to get a jump start on the growing season.

lamb's ears

Stachys byzantina 'Silver Carpet'
- Perennial
- 12-18"
- No flowers
- Zones 4-10
- Sources: b, ff

This variety has no flowers; others bear small purple blooms on silvery stalks. Less vigorous than the species. Requires well-drained soil; drought tolerant.

showy stonecrop

Hylotelephium spectabile
- Perennial
- 18-24"
- Late summer, early fall
- Pink
- Zones 4-9
- Sun
- Sources: b, q, ii

Multiseason interest; neat, succulent foliage. Let seed heads remain on plant in winter. Very easy to grow.

salvia

Salvia guaranitica
- Perennial
- 3-5'
- Late summer, fall
- Blue
- Zones 9-10
- Sources: i, u

Good late bloomer. Often treated as an annual in colder climates. Despite its blue color, this plant attracts hummingbirds well.

martagon lily

Lilium martagon
- Bulb
- 4-6'
- Early summer, summer
- Fragrant
- White to purple
- Sun, part shade
- Zones 3-8
- Sources: dd, gg, ii

Easy once established; should be in more gardens. Up to 50 sweetly scented flowers on a plant. Several named varieties are available.

korean spice viburnum

Viburnum carlesii 'Compactum'
- Shrub
- 30-42"
- Late spring
- Fragrant
- White, pink buds
- Zones 4-7
- Sun
- Sources: e, n, y

Exceptional variety; nice shape. Good near walkways.

dooryard

garden

a dooryard garden is enjoyed and shared by everyone. A garden, such as this one in Seattle, with heady fragrance, lush texture, and gorgeous color, delights the senses of visitors and passersby. Beginning at the front porch steps, the garden rambles its way toward the sidewalk—an unspoken invitation to revel in nature's bounty. Along the street, the flowers growing through the fence hint at what's on the other side: the most glorious of all possible welcomes.

The picket fence provides support for the valerian growing through it. *Opposite:* Peony-flowered poppy.

creating a dooryard entry

this dooryard garden in Seattle, Washington, tends to invite in all who pass by. Betty and Reimert Ravenholt created a flower-filled welcome in their garden by combining fragrant and colorful perennials, annuals, and roses in an informal manner. Roses climb toward the sky, flowers tumble and sway happily, and thick, lush groundcovers spill over the walkways.

No big, solid blocks of color exist to suggest a formal garden. In fact, just the opposite occurs. Dots of color, such as blue foxglove and purple delphinium, poke up through red valerian.

The garden's country-fresh look appears to have been created by nature's guiding hand instead of by the couple's personal choices. Rose and blue flowers stand out, while yellow and white blooms echo the cheerful color scheme of the house.

In effect, the garden becomes the front room of the house. The brick walk, which Reimert built, begins at the front gate and invites you to meander through the flower beds. 'Silver Mound' artemisia, pinks, and fragrant garland flowers that hug the brick edge further accentuate the easygoing walkway. Nearby flowerbeds riot with color—annual white nicotiana, cosmos, and larkspur cavort with perennial "Moonbeam' coreopsis, calla lilies, and Japanese anemones.

Country architectural details marry the landscape to the house. A red valerian-festooned picket fence, also designed and built by Reimert, frames the friendly setting. Perky English window boxes, filled to the brim with marigolds, accent the early 1900s cottage. The stepping stones, edged with woolly thyme, veer from the main path toward the side entrance.

Gardening is the Ravenholts' ultimate relaxation and creative exercise. The result draws visitors in visually (and physically, too!) to take in the textures, colors, and juxtapositions of plants and fragrances.

The Ravenholts learned the love of gardening from their families. Betty's great-grandmother was weeding, watering, and cutting flowers into her nineties. Reimert's mother passed on the love and skill of flower arranging to all of her eight children. Now, they can pass on their flower-filled legacy to their own children.

DOORYARD PLANTINGS

Nothing makes a greater first impression than a well-landscaped front yard and entryway. And, dooryard gardens effectively and aesthetically join the landscape to a home's exterior. A preponderance of perennial flowers, most of which loyally return each year, helps make the garden easy to maintain.

There are a few must-have plants for dooryard plantings. Fragrant roses are essential—climbing as well as old-fashioned shrub varieties. Daylilies and veronicas are colorful, reliable perennials. Also include some annuals, such as cosmos, zinnias, salvias, and snapdragons. Don't forget to add some trees and shrubs—structure that visually anchors the landscape.

Soften the formality of a brick walkway; let plants spill out of the beds. *Opposite:* Overview of the garden.

The joy of finally having their own property to garden.

Betty and Reimert Ravenholt spent years in a condominium in Maryland, yearning for a place and a fantasy garden of their own. Finally, they bought a dilapidated house with well-worn front yard in Seattle, Washington. Still, they were elated, as they owned a little plot, 30 × 50 feet, to make their own. After five years of hard work and experimentation, they now have a garden that stretches from the porch to the white picket fence and beyond. They designed it to be warm and welcoming for their own personal enjoyment and for that of friends and neighbors.

astilbe

Astilbe x *arendsii*
'Weisse Gloria'
- Perennial
- 2'
- Spring, summer
- Creamy-white
- Zones 4-8
- Part shade, sun
- Sources: y, aa, gg

Ferny, attractive leaves. Performs well in shady borders with rich, moist, well-drained soil.

rose campion

Lychnis coronaria
'Alba'
- Perennial
- 18-36"
- Summer
- White

- Zones 3-10
- Sun
- Sources: dd, ff

Silvery-white, woolly leaves; blends with most plants. Self-sows readily; spreads. Easy to grow even in poor soil. In ancient times the flowers were used for garlands and crowns.

lithodora

Lithodora diffusa
'Grace Ward'
- Perennial, evergreen
- 6"
- Azure blue
- Late spring-summer
- Zones 6-10
- Sun
- Sources: e, g, ii

Low-growing, clump-forming, evergreen groundcover with dark foliage. Long-lasting flowers. Prefers acid, moist, well-drained soil.

blue oat grass

Helictotrichon sempervirens
- Perennial, grass
- 1-4'
- Foliage plant
- Gray-blue

- Zones 4-8
- Sun
- Sources: e, ii

Ornamental grass with round clumps of silvery, blue-green, stiff evergreen leaves. Needs well-drained soil; avoid soggy sites.

spike speedwell

Veronica spicata
'Icicle'
- Perennial
- 18-24"
- Summer
- White
- Zones 5-8
- Sun
- Sources: e, ii

Finest white-flowered veronica; long-blooming. Good cut flowers. Vigorous; glossy green leaves. Attracts bees.

garland flower

Daphne cneorum
'Eximia'
- Shrub
- 6-12"
- Spring
- Fragrant
- Rose-pink
- Zones 4-7
- Part shade, sun
- Sources: y, bb

Stunning in flower; very fragrant. Needs well-drained soil; finicky.

mealy cup sage

Salvia farinacea 'Stratta'
- Perennial (tender)
- 14-18"

- Summer
- Blue with white
- Zones 9-10
- Sun
- Source: dd

Attractive, compact plant. Usually grown as an annual. Silvery effect from calyces.

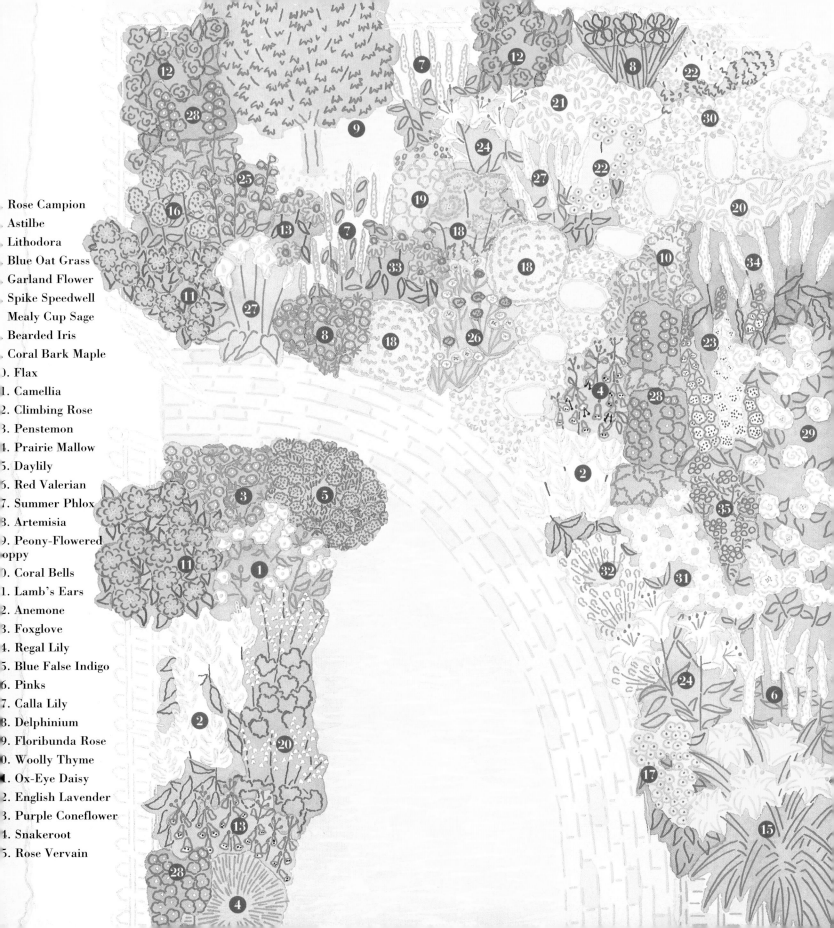

1. Rose Campion
2. Astilbe
3. Lithodora
4. Blue Oat Grass
5. Garland Flower
6. Spike Speedwell
7. Mealy Cup Sage
8. Bearded Iris
9. Coral Bark Maple
10. Flax
11. Camellia
12. Climbing Rose
13. Penstemon
14. Prairie Mallow
15. Daylily
16. Red Valerian
17. Summer Phlox
18. Artemisia
19. Peony-Flowered
Poppy
20. Coral Bells
21. Lamb's Ears
22. Anemone
23. Foxglove
24. Regal Lily
25. Blue False Indigo
26. Pinks
27. Calla Lily
28. Delphinium
29. Floribunda Rose
30. Woolly Thyme
31. Ox-Eye Daisy
32. English Lavender
33. Purple Coneflower
34. Snakeroot
35. Rose Vervain

bearded iris

Iris germanica hyb.
- Bulb
- 16-40"
- Spring, early summer
- White to purple
- Zones 3-10
- Sun
- Sources: f, n, v, ii

Easy to grow in very well-drained soil. Plant rhizome high (visible) in direction of desired growth. Divide in fall, when sparse flowering dictates the necessity.

flax

Linum perenne
- Perennial
- 1-2'
- Late spring, summer
- Pale blue
- Zones 5-10
- Sun
- Sources: f, v

Delicate, wiry stems; blue-green leaves. Good for meadow and informal gardens. Self-sows. 'Sapphire hybrids' have darker flowers.

coral bark maple

Acer palmatum 'Sango Kaku'
- 15-20'
- Foliage and bark
- Zones 5-8
- Sun
- Sources: a, e, g, y, gg

Bark is brilliant orange-red color in winter months. Bright green leaves have striking red margin in spring; turn golden yellow in fall.

camellia

Camellia sasanqua hyb.
- Shrub, tender
- 6-15'
- Late spring, summer
- Zones 7-9
- Sun
- Sources: g, n, o, y

Broad, densely-branched, pyramidal, broadleaf evergreen; dark green lustrous leaves. Bold, 2- to 3-inch flowers. Many color forms. In cold areas, grow in containers and bring indoors for winter.

climbing rose

Rosa 'American Beauty'
- Shrub
- 8-12'
- Summer
- Fragrant
- Carmine
- Zones 6-9
- Sun
- Source: x

Hybrid perpetual rose that looks like a modern tea rose. Carmine, high-centered flowers are good for cutting. Reblooms, but not continuously.

prairie mallow

Sidalcea malviflora
- Perennial
- 2-4'
- Summer
- Pink to lilac
- Zones 5-10
- Sun, part shade
- Source: ff

Mini-hollyhock in erect narrow clumps; long-blooming 1-inch flowers. Many varieties available. Cut back after flowering. Easy to grow.

penstemon

Penstemon hyb.
- Perennial
- 1-4'
- Late spring, summer
- White to red
- Zones 3-10
- Sun
- Sources: e, y, bb

Beautiful plant; attracts hummingbirds. Very cold hardy; tolerates hot summers. Grow in sand or a rock garden in full sun.

daylily

Hemerocallis 'Stella de Oro'
- Perennial
- 1-2'
- Early summer, repeats
- Yellow
- Zones 3-10
- Sun, part shade
- Sources: e, aa, ee, ii

Compact. Long-blooming with dainty, cheery yellow blooms. Edible flowers. Prefers rich, well-drained soils. Divide every 3 to 5 years.

summer phlox

Phlox paniculata 'Bright Eyes'
- Perennial
- 2-3'
- Summer
- Pink with rose
- Zones 3-9
- Sun
- Sources: gg, ii

Mildew resistant. Divide every 2 or 3 years to maintain vigor.

red valerian

Centranthus ruber
- Perennial
- 18-36"
- Carmine, rose-pink
- Zones 4-10
- Sun, part shade
- Sources: e, f, v, ii

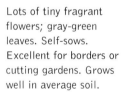

Lots of tiny fragrant flowers; gray-green leaves. Self-sows. Excellent for borders or cutting gardens. Grows well in average soil.

artemisia

Artemisia 'Silver Mound'
- Perennial
- 1'
- Foliage plant
- Silver foliage
- Zones 4-9
- Sun
- Sources: b, r, ii

Mound of silvery foliage. Trim for a neat appearance; cut down in spring. Grow in lean soil and full sun only.

peony-flowered poppy

Papaver somniferum hyb.
- Annual
- 3-4'
- Summer
- White to red

- Sun
- Sources: dd, gg

Also known as breadbox poppy. Sow seeds in the garden in late fall; or, you can sow them on top of snow in winter. Singles, doubles, and other forms available.

coral bells

Heuchera 'June Bride'
- Perennial
- 1-2'
- Spring, summer
- White
- Zones 3-10
- Sun, part shade
- Sources: e, ii

Many tall, loose spikes of plentiful white flowers over nice, scalloped foliage. Grows best in organic, well-drained soils.

lamb's ears

Stachys byzantina 'Silver Carpet'
- Perennial
- 12-18"
- Foliage plant
- Silvery leaves
- Zones 4-10
- Sun
- Sources: b, ff

Nonflowering form of lamb's ears. Not as vigorous as pink flowered species and other forms. Soft, furry leaves beg to be touched.

anemone

Anemone tomentosa
- Perennial
- 3-4'
- Summer, late summer
- Pink

- Zones 3-4
- Sun, part shade
- Source: ii

Earlier flowering than other anemones; many 2- to 3-inch flowers. Attractive foliage. 'Robustissima' is the best of the named variety.

foxglove

Digitalis purpurea
'Glittering Prizes'
- Biennial
- 4-6'
- Early summer
- White to purple
- Zones 4-8
- Part shade, sun
- Source: dd

Old garden favorites. Prefers rich, well-drained soil. Sow seed in August for bloom the following summer. Self-sows once established.

blue false indigo

Baptisia australis
- Perennial
- 3-4'
- Early summer
- Blue
- Zones 3-10
- Sun, part shade
- Sources: e, f, v, ii

Very ornamental, blue-green foliage. Erect stems with 1-inch indigo blue flowers; handsome seed pods. Easy to grow.

regal lily

Lilium regale
- Bulb
- 4-6'
- Summer
- Fragrant
- White with rose buds
- Zones 3-9
- Sun
- Sources: dd, gg

Magnificent, large perfumed trumpets; up to 30 per plant. Needs staking. Comes back for many years. Grows best in average, well-drained soil.

pinks

Dianthus chinensis hyb.
- Annual
- 12-18"
- Summer
- Fragrant
- White to lilac
- Zones 7-10
- Sun
- Source: z

Clove-scented, edible flowers on erect, stiff stems. Grow in shade where summers are hot. Wide range of single color and bicolored varieties.

calla lily

Zantedeschia aethiopica
- Bulb, tender
- 3'
- Summer
- White
- Zones 8-10
- Sun
- Sources: j, n

Large, sensuous flowers. Start indoors in March; set outdoors after last frost; store indoors for winter.

delphinium

*Delphinium
grandiflorum*
'Tom Thumb'
- Perennial
- 12-18"
- Blue
- Zones 3-10
- Sun
- Source: ff

Short-lived. Sometimes
treated as annual; can
flower from early
sowing first year.

woolly thyme

*Thymus
pseudolanuginosus*
- Perennial, herb
- 1"
- Spring
- Fragrant

- Pale mauve
- Zones 5-9
- Sun
- Sources: f, v

Wonderful little ground-
cover thyme; fuzzy
gray-green leaves. A
good groundcover to
plant between stepping
stones. Requires well-
drained, lean soil.

floribunda rose

osa 'Iceberg'
Shrub
4'
Summer
Fragrant
White
Zones 5-7
Sun
Source: x

pright, bushy form.
ragrant blooms in
usters all season.
usceptible to
ackspot.

ox-eye daisy

Leucanthemum vulgare
(*Chrysanthemum
leucanthemum*)
- Perennial
- 12-24"
- Early summer
- White
- Zones 3-10
- Sun
- Sources: v, z

Forms low, spreading
mats of deep-green
leaves. Cheery white,
yellow-eyed flowers.

english lavender

Lavandula angustifolia
(*Lavandula vera*)
- Shrub
- 3-4'
- Spring
- Fragrant
- Purple
- Zones 5-8
- Sun
- Sources: f, o, v, z, dd

Aromatic silver-gray
foliage; fragrant
flowers. Cut back for
rebloom. Grows in any
well-drained soil.

purple coneflower

Echinacea purpurea
- Perennial
- 3-4'
- Summer
- Purple
- Zones 3-10
- Sun
- Sources: q, u, gg

Easy North American
native with 3-inch,
daisylike flowers;
attracts butterflies.
Prefers sunny, well-
drained spot. Deadhead
spent flowers for
continuous bloom. In
late summer, stop
cutting the flowers;
allow seedheads to
ripen. They'll attract
birds in fall and winter.

snakeroot

Cimicifuga racemosa
- Perennial
- 4-6'
- Summer
- Fragrant
- White
- Zones 3-10
- Part shade, sun
- Sources: v, ii, jj

Native plant with
handsome, divided, dark
green leaves. Tall, wiry
stems. Attractive fall
fruits.

rose vervain

Verbena canadensis
- Perennial
- 6-8"
- Purple to pink
- Summer-fall
- Zones 5-10
- Sun
- Source: e

Showy, large flower
clusters. Flops, so use
over walls and in
containers. Often grown
as annual.

coastal

garden

the seaside cottage called out for a garden—one to withstand salt air, wind, and rain. Deep blue, pink, orange, yellow, and scarlet flowers produce an enchanted medley. Ordered, yet carefree, borders of pine trees, shrubs, and ferns barely contain a profusion of nasturtiums, marguerites, dahlias, coreopsis, lobelias, phlox, calendulas, godetias, cosmos, and more flowers.

Vivid nasturtiums, dahlias, lilies, and rose campion are softened by coastal mists. *Opposite*: Gladiola.

this small and intimate planting is a classic cottage garden, Pacific Northwest style. The garden's lush and sturdy appearance today denies its humble beginning.

There wasn't much to see when June and Les Kroft arrived to remodel their Oregon seaside cottage for year-round use. The cottage and outbuildings occupied two-thirds of the 50 × 100-foot lot. No garden existed. The lawn, a swampy area of ground prone to flooding, was filled with construction debris, old lumber, and gravel. To make matters worse, wind constantly swept the open lot.

With only about 175 feet between them and the ocean, the Krofts knew they'd have to carefully plan, select, and plant durable, salt- and wind-tolerant varieties. Les's death shortly after their arrival left June to fulfill their shared vision.

As the project began, June discovered that she needed a new set of rules to garden by the sea. Frequent flooding, caused by a high water table, necessitated the installation of a series of drainage ditches and background for tall perennials. Slowly a garden space evolved.

Topping the ditches with gravel turned them into wandering garden paths. Then June used spare lumber from the cottage renovation to build raised planting beds. Decorative (but very utilitarian) fences served as windbreaks.

June loosened and lightened the clay soil by adding a mixture of compost, peat moss, and sand. The foot-high planting beds required soil leftover from the renovation excavations as well as soil June carted home from plentiful molehills in nearby fields.

Then the magic began. On completing the basics, June started planting by scattering seeds throughout the beds—a lighthearted approach. She and gardening friends shared cuttings along with leftover seed and divided plants. She planted pine tree varieties and small, tough shrubs—the most durable, salt-tolerant varieties were planted around the perimeters of the garden, with the less resistant cultivars in the center.

A painter and quilter, June gardens with the eye of an artist. The garden's composition reflects her background and her love of mixing colors. She explores and exploits every tone, texture, and shade, from the smallest dab of color to big, bold strokes.

Salt Tolerance

One of the challenges to gardening near the ocean is finding plants that will tolerate the continuous salt spray. And, depending on how far away you are from the water's edge, there is always the danger of flooding from high tides.

You can grow annuals and perennials as well as trees for seaside areas that are quite salt tolerant, such as Sycamore maple (*Acer pseudoplatanus*), many spruce (*Picea* spp.), and pines (*Pinus* spp.).

Salt-tolerant shrubs, such as shadbush (*Amelanchier canadensis*), beach rose (*Rosa rugosa*), junipers (*Juniperus* spp.), lavender cotton (*Santolina chamaecyparissus*), and Virginia sweetspire (*Itea virginica*), also contribute to the diversity of a seaside garden.

a garden by the seaside

Like the tides, bright borders ebb and flow with

color. Soft, muted tones abound in coastal Oregon. Salt-spray battered cottages blend softly into a monochromatic palette. Just beyond a tidy picket fence, a splash of color suddenly appears. A painted metal sign triumphantly announces visitors' arrival to June Kroft's garden.

Nasturtiums started it all—ones like her Aunt Ella grew. June loved everything about them—the scent, color, shape of their leaves—as well as making tasty nasturtium sandwiches. And, because they grew so well, she gained the confidence to create and grow the garden she envisioned.

summer phlox

Phlox paniculata
'Starfire'
- Perennial
- 2-3'
- Summer
- Fragrant
- Cherry-red
- Zones 3-9
- Sun
- Sources: b, ii

Blooms earlier than other varieties. Prefers deep, rich soil.

loosestrife

Lythrum virgatum
'Morden Pink'
- Perennial
- 42"
- Summer
- Magenta
- Zones 3-10
- Sun, part shade

- Source: ff

Valuable border plant. Vigorous, upright, very free blooming. Non-invasive; prefers damp soils.

tiger lily

Lilium lancifolium
(Lilium tigrinum)
- Bulb
- 3-5'
- Late summer
- Red-orange with black spots
- Zones 2-9

- Sun
- Source: ii

Easy-to-grow garden favorite. Up to 40 flowers per bulb. Don't plant near other lilies; it can transmit a virus. Many black bulbils along stem can be planted. Prefers well-drained, organic soil.

calendula

Calendula officinalis
hyb.
- Annual
- 18"
- Summer to fall
- Yellow to orange
- Sun
- Sources: f, v, dd

Also called pot marigold. Useful plant for drying, culinary purposes, ornamental, crafts, dyes, and cosmetics. Edible flowers. Many attractive varieties. Easy to grow in average soils.

nasturtium

Tropaeolum majus
Alaska Hybrids
- Annual
- 12-18"
- Summer
- Yellow, orange
- Sun
- Sources: r, z, cc, dd

Variegated foliage; edible flowers. Likes cool weather; sow early in garden. Easy to grow in lean soils.

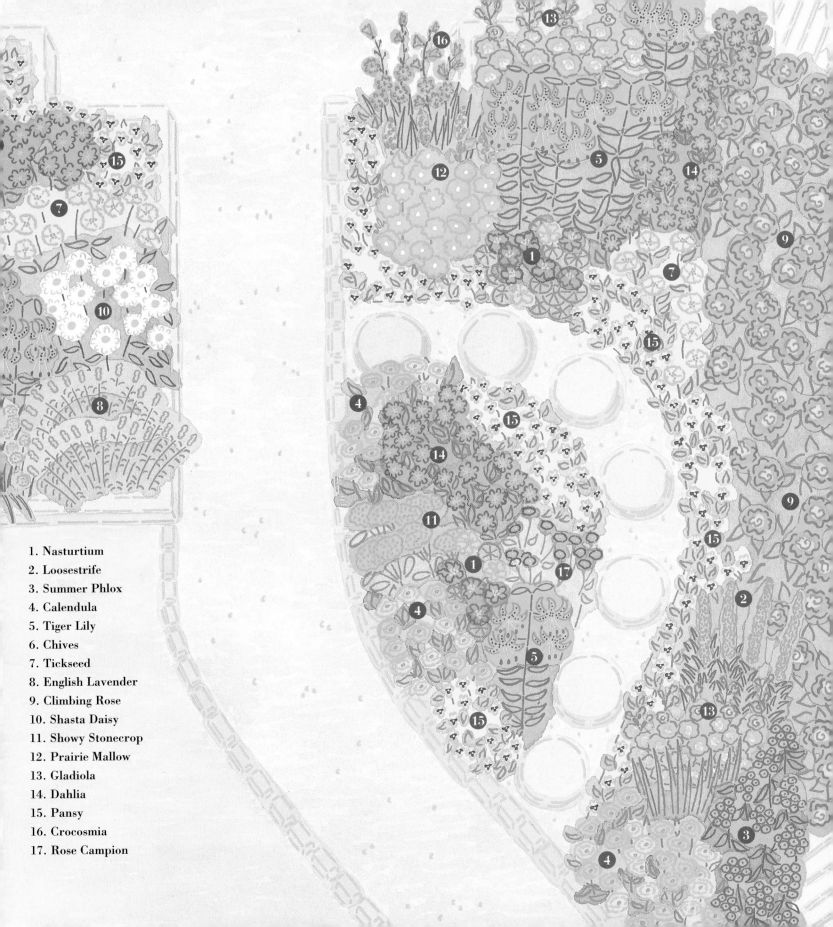

1. Nasturtium
2. Loosestrife
3. Summer Phlox
4. Calendula
5. Tiger Lily
6. Chives
7. Tickseed
8. English Lavender
9. Climbing Rose
10. Shasta Daisy
11. Showy Stonecrop
12. Prairie Mallow
13. Gladiola
14. Dahlia
15. Pansy
16. Crocosmia
17. Rose Campion

chives

Allium schoenoprasum
- Perennial, herb
- 18″
- Early summer
- Blue-purple
- Zones 3-10
- Sun
- Sources: j, t, hh

Wonderful ornamental with edible leaves and flowers; belongs in every garden. Shear after flowering. Pest free.

tickseed

Coreopsis grandiflora
- Perennial
- 1-3′
- Early summer, summer
- Yellow
- Zones 4-10
- Sun, part shade
- Sources: e, gg

Many 2-inch, bright-yellow flowers; long-flowering. Excellent for cutting. Deadhead for continuous bloom.

english lavender

Lavandula angustifolia (Lavandula vera)
- Shrub, herb
- 3-4′
- Spring
- Fragrant
- Lilac

- Zones 5-8
- Sun
- Sources: f, o, v, z, dd

For border or herb garden, any well-drained soil. Aromatic silver-gray foliage; fragrant flowers good for cutting or drying. Cut back for rebloom. Drought resistant.

climbing rose

Rosa 'Joseph's Coat'
- Shrub
- 8-10′
- Summer, early fall
- Fragrant
- Yellow into red
- Zones 5-9
- Sun
- Source: gg

Strong, upright climber. Double flowers change color daily (yellow into red). Reblooms.

shasta daisy

Leucanthemum x *superbum* 'Shasta Snow' (*Chrysanthemum* x *superbum*)
- Perennial
- White with yellow
- 1-3′
- Summer
- Zones 5-10
- Sun, part shade
- Sources: cc, gg

Popular, easy plant with long-blooming season. Prefers well-drained, organic soil. Divide every few years.

showy stonecrop

Hylotelephium (Sedum) 'Autumn Joy'

- Perennial
- 24-30″
- Late summer, early fall
- Pink, then rose
- Zones 3-9
- Sun

- Sources: g, n, u

Neat, succulent foliage. Clusters of starry flowers resemble pink broccoli. Three-season interest; don't cut back in autumn, allow seed heads to remain through winter. Needs well-drained soil.

prairie mallow

Sidalacea malviflora
- Perennial
- 2-4′
- Summer
- Pink
- Zones 5-10
- Sun, part shade
- Sources: b, e, ii

Long-blooming, 1-inch flowers resemble small hollyhocks. Cut back after flowering. May need staking.

gladiola

Gladiolus hyb.
- Bulb
- 2-3′
- Summer
- White to purple
- Zones 7-10
- Sun
- Sources: b, t, hh

Showy in the garden and as cut flowers; wide variety of colors. Dig up in fall and store indoors in cold winter areas. Stagger plantings for longest bloom.

dahlia

Dahlia 'Figaro'
- Bulb, tender
- 12"
- Summer-frost
- Yellow to red
- Zones 7-10
- Sun, part shade
- Source: dd

Dwarf series with single and double flowers; many colors. Stake at planting. Good for the front of border or containers. In cold winter areas, dig tubers in fall and store indoors.

crocosmia

Crocosmia 'James Coey'
- Bulb
- 18-36"
- Late summer, early fall
- Orange-red
- Zones 6-10
- Sun
- Source: d

Elegant clumps of sword-shaped leaves. Large flowers on arching spikes. Good as a colorful accent or as a mass planting. Pest resistant.

pansy

Viola x *wittrockiana*
Bingo Hybrids
- Annual
- 8"
- Yellow with burgundy
- Part shade
- Source: b

Perky blooms; edible flowers. Start seed 12 weeks before spring frost-free date. Or, plant in fall for autumn bloom; will stay through winter to bloom again in spring. Prefers moist, organic soil.

rose campion

Lychnis coronaria
- Perennial
- 18-36"
- Summer
- Magenta
- Zones 3-10
- Sun
- Sources: e, j, z

Bright accent; vividly colored flowers contrast with silvery-woolly leaves. Spreading. Grows best in poor soils; short-lived, but self-sows.

tall

borders

a Massachusetts garden reaches for the sky. Regal spires of blossoms rise upward; wide drifts of flowers provide depth and richness. The summer garden reaches its colorful peak as large patches of luminous garden loosestrife, globe thistle, and rose campion soar skyward. They gently sway in the soft coastal breezes as pastel foxgloves, 8 feet high, catch the eye. Tall borders demand attention—and get it!

Foxgloves, often used as background plants, define these borders' edges. *Opposite*: Garden loosestrife.

Yellow garden loosestrife and blue speedwell are stunning bed-fellows. *Opposite:* Garden overview.

t he first things Harold and Julia Pierce put in their new garden were two climbing 'Joseph's Coat' roses to clamber up a stately trellis. The gray wooden structure enhances the garden's design and provides winter interest.

Clematis, pyracantha, and more roses stretch for the sky, while a neatly trimmed, dwarf boxwood hedge acts as a diminutive counterpoint.

The enriched soil produces the nutrients that support these tall plants and stimulate them to multiply and set seed. Harold and Julia work loads of decomposed leaves from the local recycling program into the garden each year. In addition, they fertilize every few weeks. This successful renewal is ongoing.

Volunteers—self-sown plants—are encouraged and given special attention. The massive patch that now has over 500 foxgloves was started with the gift of a few plants from a neighbor. Along with "nature's seeding," the Pierces painstakingly collect seed each year, dry it in the sun, and scatter it over partially shaded, moist soil in August. They put down a layer of salt hay to protect the plants in winter, then move them to permanent locations in the spring. They follow the same steps with rose campion, hollyhocks, and Canterbury-bells. This process results in an abundance of new, indeed lush, plantings each year.

The Pierces select plant combinations by size and with an eye to compatible colors. 'May Night' salvia works well with the golden yellow blossoms of garden loosestrife. This perennial sage more than earns its place in the garden by flowering from May through June and by blooming again after deadheading (the removal of spent flower spikes). The steel blue, 4-foot-tall globe thistle combines well with most plants. In this garden, it nicely accents the delicate pink roses with which it shares a bed. The silvery velvet leaves of rose campion blend with a myriad of plants, even as its magenta flowers make a show-stopping display. Rose campion blooms more robustly in the second year of growth, then dies out. The plant freely self-seeds to provide stock plants for future years, so it is well worth nurturing.

TALL PLANT CARE

Start early for the best results. Place stakes early in spring so as not to disturb roots. Use supports that are as thick as the plant stems and about two-thirds the height of the mature plant. Tie with natural materials such as garden twine, raffia, or grape-vine. Natural stakes, such as oak twigs or bamboo, blend well in the garden.

Stake single stems of lilies, foxgloves, and coneflowers by placing the stake a few inches behind the main stem and securing with soft twine. When the plant doubles in height, repeat the process, tying about every 10 inches.

Multiple stem staking is used for floppy plants, such as loosestrife, phlox, and salvias, that grow out and up. In late spring, encircle the plants with stakes, then weave twine around the outside of the stakes and through the clump.

tall plants add depth to a garden

Spires of foxgloves take *center stage* in late spring.

When Harold and Julia Pierce moved into their two-story New England home dating from the 1800s, they realized they couldn't change its low-slung position on the lot. Wide foundation plantings would have smothered it. So they decided to capitalize on their lot's strength and adopted a vertical design. They focused on plants that would scale walls, grow up a trellis, or naturally reach for the sky. An added benefit of vertical plantings is the fragrance they produce overhead in the garden. Aromatic climbers include autumn clematis, moonflower, honeysuckle, and many roses.

1. Bugloss
2. Ox-Eye Daisy
3. Foxglove
4. Peony
5. Japanese Black Pine
6. Speedwell
7. Nippon Daisy
8. Climbing Rose
9. Bluestar
10. Garden Loosestrife
11. Petunia
12. Floribunda Rose
13. Asiatic Lily
14. Globe Thistle
15. Garden Balsam

bugloss

Anchusa azurea hyb.
- Perennial
- 1-5′
- Early summer
- Blue
- Zones 3-10
- Sources: b, r, s, dd

Also known as alkanet. Invaluable summer color; floppy habit. Prefers deep, organic, well-drained, yet moisture-retentive soil.

ox-eye dais

Leucanthemum vulgare (*Chrysanthemum leucanthemum*)
- Perennial
- 12-24″
- Early summer
- White
- Zones 3-10
- Sun
- Sources: v, ff

Forms low mats of deep-green leaves; spreading. Cheery white, yellow-eyed flowers.

foxglove

Digitalis purpurea
- Biennial
- 4-6'
- Early summer
- White to purple, spotted
- Zones 4-8
- Part shade, sun
- Source: dd

Cottage garden favorites. Prefers rich, well-drained soil. Sow seed in August. Self-sows.

peony

Paeonia officinalis 'Don Richardson'
- Perennial
- 30-36"
- Late spring, early summer
- Fragrant
- Cherry red
- Zones 2-10
- Source: i

Japanese type with dark, cherry-red petals. Requires deep, rich, well-drained soil. Use grow-throughs for support.

japanese black pine

Pinus thunbergii
- Tree, evergreen
- 20-40'
- Foliage plant
- Dark green
- Zones 5-9
- Sources: e, g, n

Very attractive, lustrous, needled foliage. Grows best in moist, rich soil, yet tolerates sand. Good seaside plant; salt spray and drought tolerant.

speedwell

Veronica spicata hyb.
- Perennial
- 1-2'
- Summer
- Blue to red
- Zones 3-10
- Part shade
- Sources: b, z, dd

Dense plants covered with little flowers on tapering spikes; long-blooming. Easy to grow.

nippon daisy

Nipponanthemum nipponicum (Chrysanthemum nipponicum)
- Perennial
- 30-36"
- Fall-frost
- White
- Zones 5-10
- Sun
- Sources: c, e, v

Large, shrublike. Cut near ground in early spring and pinch back twice more.

climbing rose

Rosa 'Joseph's Coat'
- Shrub
- 8-10'
- Summer, early fall
- Fragrant
- Yellow into red
- Zones 5-9

- Sun
- Source: gg

Vigorous, upright climber. Double flowers change color—yellow into red; good rebloom. Disease resistant.

bluestar

Amsonia tabernaemontana
- Perennial
- 2-3'
- Early summer
- Light blue
- Zones 3-9
- Sun, part shade
- Sources: c, n, jj

Best in moist, rich soil; low maintenance. Sear cut ends of stems when making an arrangement.

garden loosestrife

Lysimachia punctata
- Perennial
- 36"
- Summer to fall
- Yellow
- Zones 3-10
- Sun, part shade
- Sources: j, z, dd

Good in moist/wet soil, but will grow in drier soil in part shade. Deadhead to prevent self sowing.

petunia

Petunia x *hybrida*
- Annual
- 8-18"
- Summer
- Fragrant
- White to purple
- Sun
- Sources: cc, dd

Start seed early indoors or buy plants at nursery. Various colors and varieties: doubles, marked, or fringed.

floribunda rose

Rosa 'Betty Prior'
- Shrub
- 5-7'
- Spring, summer
- Fragrant
- Medium-deep pink
- Zones 5-9
- Sun
- Sources: x, gg

Abundant clusters of single flowers. Vigorous, upright. High-performance rose.

globe thistle

Echinops ritro
- Perennial
- 2-3'
- Summer
- Blue
- Zones 3-10
- Sun
- Sources: e, ii, jj

White-woolly stems and leaf reverses. Some name confusion; purchase on site. Round (globe) flower heads good as cut or dried flowers.

asiatic lily

Lilium 'Snowlark'
- Bulb
- 3-5'
- Summer
- White with maroon spots
- Zones 4-10
- Sun, part shade
- Source: ii

White lily with out-facing flowers. Perfect for an evening garden. Easy-to-grow bulbs multiply over time. Interplant with daylilies.

garden balsam

Impatiens balsamina hyb.
- Annual
- 24-30"
- Summer to fall
- White to purple
- Part shade, sun
- Sources: v, dd

More upright than regular impatiens; flowers along the stem. Many varieties; some fully double. Start seed early indoors; prefer warmth outdoors.

easy-care
garden

the lavish display of the Portland, Oregon, garden of landscape designer Steve Carruthers is actually his home proving grounds. Here, he tests ways of cutting down on garden maintenance for both himself and his clients. One approach is to reduce the number of garden chores that need to be done in spring and to spend part of that beautiful time of year savoring his country garden.

Edging plants, such as silvery lamb's ears, spill into the path and soften the hard edge of the bed. *Opposite:* Columbine.

creating the easy-care garden

oday, as Steve Carruthers walks from the patio to the backyard garden of his quarter-acre property in Portland, Oregon, it's as if he's entering a living bouquet. White, rose, and pink mounds of thrift, cranesbill geraniums, and pinks line and soften the edge of the curving beds. Foxgloves, in white, pink, and apricot, tower above late-flowering peonies. Silvery-felted mullein stand tall alongside sapphire-hued delphiniums, while love-in-a-mist seems to float like a cloud of fine, green foliage.

When Steve, a landscape designer, first built his house and started gardening, he had plenty of time for planting and tending to his garden. Now, even when his garden demands the most attention, he's working 12-hour days in other people's yards.

To deal with his crunched schedule, Steve found ways to cut down significantly on the time he needed to perform routine maintenance chores such as weeding and watering. First, he eliminated all but what he calls "high value" perennials. These perennials have long or repeat bloom periods, provide multiseason interest, tolerate drought, and are disease resistant.

Steve then took the next step, adding woody plants. He selected trees and shrubs which were both low-maintenance and colorful, including a variegated dogwood (*Cornus alba* 'Elegantissima'), 'Frost' flowering cherry, a leaf-curl-resistant peach, and golden box honeysuckle.

As fill-ins, he used reseeding annuals and biennials. For height, Steve planted foxgloves and clary sage. He sowed seeds of mountain bluets, love-in-a-mist, flowering tobacco, and fragrant wallflowers for the middle of one border. And, finally, he put in sweet alyssum, cranesbill, and dwarf lady's mantle as edgers.

Steve firmly believes in feeding the soil, which in turn feeds the plants and keeps them at peak performance. In February, before new growth starts, he spreads an inch of composted chicken manure throughout the beds. He also limes the beds, but doesn't mulch them because he wants the self-sown seeds to germinate without any interference.

MULCH MORE AND WORK LESS

Mulching saves work in several ways. A 2- to 4-inch layer of organic matter stops weed seeds from germinating. Mulch perennial beds once plants are growing strongly. Don't cover up self-sown seedlings.

Mulch also conserves soil moisture, so you don't have to water as often. With adequate moisture, your plants will be strong, healthy, and resistant to pests and disease.

Apply winter mulch, 6 to 12 inches of lightweight material, such as straw, over perennials after the ground has frozen. This keeps the plants from heaving out of the ground during freezing and thawing cycles.

Clematis is happy with its roots shaded and flowers in full sun. *Opposite*: Overview of the garden.

Take time to **watch the birds** and smell the flowers.

Portland, Oregon, artist-turned-landscape designer Steve Carruthers is a sensualist. He wants to sit in the garden, enjoy the fragrance, and take in the colors, while listening to the wind moving through the leaves. He takes time to watch birds fly in and drink from one of his handmade concrete water basins. Steve's goal is to create a place where he can relax and think freely. But he insists on a lush English cottage garden without spring's high-maintenance chores. And, most of all, his objective is to have time for new plants—unopened and unexplored gifts.

scabiosa

Scabiosa caucasica hyb.
- Perennial
- 18-30"
- Summer, late summer
- Blue

- Zones 3-10
- Sun
- Sources: gg, ii

Also known as pincushion flower. Best perennial scabiosa; many named cultivars are available. Great cut flower, fresh or air dried. Looks best when planted in groups of 3 or 5 in a border.

1. Scabiosa
2. Kaffir Lily
3. Sweet Coneflower
4. Rose Campion
5. Delphinium
6. Gayfeather
7. Arborvitae
8. Speedwell
9. Crocosmia
10. Siberian Iris
11. Beard-Tongue
12. Obedient Plant
13. Peony
14. Prairie Mallow
15. Sea Lavender
16. Cranesbill
17. Cape Fuchsia
18. Heavenly Bamboo
19. Columbine
20. Bellflower
21. Shrub Rose
22. Clary Sage
23. Golden Box Honeysuckle
24. Bugloss
25. Catmint
26. Hellebore
27. Bluebeard
28. Mountain Bluet
29. Lady's Mantle

kaffir lily

Schizostylis coccinea
- Perennial
- 1-2'
- Late summer-fall
- Red
- Zones 6-10
- Sun
- Sources: n, dd

Late season color. Sword-shaped leaves. Prefers organic, well-drained soils; mulch in summer.

rose campion

Lychnis coronaria
- Perennial
- 18-36"
- Summer
- Magenta
- Zones 3-10
- Sun

- Sources: e, j, z

Silvery-woolly leaves accented with brightly colored flowers. Grows best in poor soils. Short-lived, but readily self-sows.

sweet coneflower

Rudbeckia subtomentosa
- Perennial
- Early fall-fall
- Fragrant
- Yellow
- Zones 5-9
- Sun, part shade
- Sources: e, dd

Slightly fragrant flowers. Gray hairs on leaves and stems. Performs well in average soil in sunny spot.

delphinium

Delphinium elatum 'Pacific Giant'
- Perennial
- 5-8'
- Summer
- Blue to white
- Zones 3-10
- Sun
- Sources: b, r, s, cc, dd

Dramatic, gorgeous, finicky, but worth it. Short-lived; replace every 2 years.

gayfeather

Liatris spicata 'Kobold'
- Perennial
- 1.5-3'
- Summer, fall
- Zones 3-10
- Violet
- Sun
- Sources: e, j, ff, ii

Spiky flowers for border. Grows best in somewhat fertile soil without winter wetness.

arborvitae

Thuja occidentalis
- Tree, evergreen
- 40-60'
- Foliage plant
- Green needles
- Zones 2-8
- Sun
- Source: ff

Prefers moist, deep, organic, well-drained soil. Provide ample water during first 2 years. Protect from wind, heavy snow.

speedwell

Veronica austriaca 'Crater Lake Blue'
- Perennial
- 12"
- Spring
- Blue
- Zones 3-10
- Sun
- Sources: e, dd, ii

One of the best of the speedwells; many blue flowers. Cut back after flowering for rebloom.

crocosmia

Crocosmia 'Lucifer'
- Perennial
- 18-36"
- Late summer, early fall
- Flame red
- Zones 6-9
- Sun
- Sources: g, n, gg, ii, jj

Elegant clumps of sword-shaped leaves. Arching spike of flowers. Good as an accent plant or in a mass planting.

siberian iris

Iris siberica
- Perennial
- 24-48"
- Late spring, early summer
- White to purple
- Zones 4-10
- Sun, part shade
- Source: j

Elegant, with upright foliage. Easy-to-grow plant that can take tough conditions. Prefers well-drained, organic soils.

obedient plant

Physostegia virginiana
- Perennial
- 3'
- Summer-fall
- Pink
- Zones 3-10
- Sun, part shade
- Sources: n, dd

Perfect for a border or cutting garden; long blooming. 'Summer Snow' has white flowers and dark green foliage; blooms in midsummer.

beard-tongue

Penstemon 'Sour Grapes'
- Perennial
- 2-3'
- Summer
- Purple with white
- Zones 7-10
- Sun
- Sources: e, i, bb

Showy; the perfect penstemon for a border. Forms bushy clumps with erect stems. Prefers well-drained soil.

peony

Paeonia lactiflora
'Legion of Honor'
- Perennial
- 32"
- Late spring, early summer
- Fragrant
- Scarlet red
- Zones 2-10
- Sun
- Source: l

Upright, lime-green foliage. Highly fragrant, single flowers. Prefers deep, rich soil. Doesn't like to be moved.

prairie mallow

Sidalcea malviflora 'Party Girl'
- Perennial
- 2-4'
- Summer
- Pink
- Zones 5-10
- Part shade/sun
- Sources: b, dd, ii

Tall with many small flowers held above foliage. Prefers sun, but will perform decently in moist, shady spot.

cranesbill

Geranium x oxonianum 'Claridge Druce'
- Perennial
- 3', spread to 3'
- Late spring-late summer
- Rose
- Zones 4-9
- Sun, part shade
- Source: i

Wonderful plant with deeply divided, gray-green leaves. Vigorous enough for ground-cover use.

sea lavender

Limonium latifolium
- Perennial
- 24"
- Summer, late summer
- Lavender blue
- Zones 3-10
- Sun
- Sources: j, r, s, v, dd

Lots of tiny flowers in an airy mass; great for drying. Easy to grow in well-drained soil; salt tolerant.

cape fuchsia

Phygelius capensis
- Perennial
- Summer-fall
- Red to orange
- Zones 7-10
- Sun
- Sources: e, f, dd

Loose bunches of 2-inch long flowers provide continuous bloom. Cut back for compact shape. Grows best in light soil; needs moisture during growing season.

heavenly bamboo

Nandina domestica
- Shrub
- 6-8'
- Late spring, early summer
- White
- Zones 6-9
- Sun to shade
- Sources: e, g, n, y

Bamboolike leaves. Gorgeous red berries.

columbine

Aquilegia alpina
- Perennial
- 12-30"
- Spring-summer
- Blue, blue with white
- Zones 3-10
- Sun, part shade
- Sources: t, v, aa

Attractive plant with nodding flowers; slightly grayed foliage. Must have good drainage.

bellflower

Campanula latifolia
- Perennial
- 3-4'
- Summer
- Blue, white
- Zones 3-10
- Sun, part shade

- Source: y

Big, bold plant forms; sturdy, erect clumps. Easy to grow. Short-lived. Several outstanding varieties. 'Macrantha' is a darker blue, and 'Alba' has white flowers.

shrub rose

Rosa 'Belle Story'
- Shrub
- 3', 6' spread
- Late spring-summer
- Fragrant
- Silvery pink
- Zones 5-9
- Sources: x, gg

A David Austin, modern hybrid rose that looks and smells like an old-fashioned variety. Small sprays of very fragrant flowers. Reblooms. Needs little pruning.

clary sage

Salvia sclarea
- Biennial
- 3-5'
- Spring, summer
- Fragrant
- White and blue
- Zones 5-9
- Sun
- Sources: f, r, v

Popular, attractive herb with large leaves and 1-inch flowers. Aromatic, medicinal smell. Self-sows.

golden box honeysuckle

Lonicera nitida 'Baggesen's Gold'
- Perennial
- 4-6'
- Spring
- White
- Zones 6-9
- Sun

- Sources: g, u, y

Golden leaves; color fades with time. Cooler conditions favor better color. Mounded (haystack) habit.

bugloss

Anchusa azurea
- Perennial
- 3-5'
- Early summer
- Blue
- Zones 3-8
- Sources: b, r, dd

Also known as alkanet. Invaluable; blue summer color. Floppy habit; may be caged or loosely hoop-staked. Prefers deep, organic, well-drained, moisture-retentive soil.

catmint

Nepeta x faassenii 'Blue Wonder'
- Perennial
- 1'
- Summer
- Lavender-blue
- Zones 3-10
- Sun
- Source: g

Gray-leafed, durable plant. Good for edging beds or borders. Prefers well-drained soil. Cut back for rebloom and to prevent self-sowing.

hellebore

Helleborus argutifolius
(Helleborus corsicus)
- Perennial
- 1-2'
- Late winter, spring
- Apple green
- Zones 6-9
- Part shade
- Sources: g, y, dd

Bushy clumps of blue-green leaves. Apple-green flowers start in winter in mild areas; may last into summer. Poisonous.

mountain bluet

Centaurea montana
- Perennial
- 1-3'
- Early summer-early fall
- Blue
- Zones 3-10
- Sun, part shade
- Sources: e, s, v, dd, ii

Very long-blooming plant; 2- to 3-inch flowers. Makes a good filler. Self-sows, which can be a problem in good soil.

bluebeard

Caryopteris x clandonensis
- Shrub
- 3-5'
- Summer
- Blue
- Zones 5-9
- Sun, part shade
- Sources: a, g, n, y, ff

Treat it as a perennial; cut down to several inches above ground level in early spring, as it blooms on new wood. Prefers well-drained soil.

lady's mantle

Alchemilla mollis
- Perennial
- 1-2'
- Late spring, early summer
- Chartreuse
- Zones 3-9
- Sun
- Sources: y, gg, ii

Ornamental, scalloped shaped, gray-green leaves look like an opened cloak (lady's mantle). Airy flowers are good for cutting or drying.

roadside
border

Cut faded flowers of 'Blaze' rose and it will keep blooming. *Opposite*: 'Nicki Red' flowering tobacco.

big, beautiful, and bodacious best describe this northern California garden. It grabs the attention of various passersby driving down the road. The design was key to the success of this garden. Big clumps of stair-stepped perennials, with annuals giving a lift during lulls, are bold enough to be glimpsed even from a car passing at 50 miles per hour. Brilliant masses of color—orange, blue, and yellow—tempt hurried drivers to slow down and turn into the vineyard.

The Cakebread family's garden, located in Brentwood in the wine country of northern California, was designed to serve several purposes. Dolores

vineyard). This produced a light soil that was well drained, yet provided adequate nutrients for long-blooming plants.

A rectangular, geometric border allows a more carefree planting style. Structure is defined and contained by the perimeters, but softened by the boldness

the border. Dolores grew annuals, such as marigolds and salvias, along with bulbs, such as daffodils, gladiolus, tulips, and iris, to keep the border exciting and

She uses her edible flowers for tea sandwiches or hors d'oeuvres to accompany wines. Roses, nasturtiums, daylilies, calendulas, and pansies are all part of her culinary repertory.

Scent is not neglected either. Dolores plants

PLANT PLACEMENT

In the Cakebread family's border, the existing trees became part of the plan, providing a sense of structure. Even in the beginning, the border seemed mature.

You, too, can use trees or large shrubs pruned into tree form in small-scale borders. They add important texture, scale, and interest.

a coloful vineyard garden

Cakebread wanted the roadside border to be bold and splashy, yet the flowers had to be utilitarian. For her, that meant a mixture of different plants, some of which have flowers that are good for cutting and using in arrangements, others that are delicious and edible.

Before any planting could begin, Dolores prepared the beds. She fortified the earth with topsoil and chicken manure that had been composted with heat-treated grape skins (they have a lot of them at the

and fun within.

In this garden, clumps of plants allow for playful mixing of colors and integrating bold colors throughout the beds. The result is exuberant rather than rigid, yet grabs your attention immediately. The layout also permits each plant to fully show off during its moment in the sun and not be blocked from view by another.

In the early years of

varied throughout the long growing season. Today, her focus has changed, and perennials now color most of the border. Dolores still includes some annuals to give those needed exclamation points of color or, as necessary, fill-ins late in the season.

nose-pleasing favorites for informal bouquets. Stock and flowering tobacco are fragrant at night, even when cut. Iceland poppies, calendulas, roses, beard-tongue, foxgloves, and delphinium all find a place in Dolores's country bouquets.

It's wise to plan before you plant. In a border, which is viewed from one side, the varying heights of flowers and plants dictate placing the tallest at the back and the smallest in front.

Plant individual varieties of annuals and perennials in free-form drifts (not soldierly rows) of three, five, seven, or any odd number that you prefer and your budget allows. Don't use even numbers of plants, as they are not as pleasing to the eye.

The bold color combination of golden calendulas and purple alyssum. *Opposite:* Overview of the garden.

They knew that **big and bold** plantings were key

to getting noticed. When the Cakebreads started their northern California vineyard, they had no budget for massive signs or elegant tasting rooms. Dolores began work on her eye-catching garden, an ambitious L-shaped border that now measures 110 feet along the main road and edges 196 feet of driveway. She hoped those large, bright masses of color would capture the attention of passing motorists, and they did. The Cakebreads' flowers are now a friendly invitation to stop and admire the gardens. They also encourage people to sample and buy wine.

beard-tongue

Penstemon
'Scarlet Queen'
- Perennial
- 2'
- Summer
- Red with white
- Zones 7-9
- Sun
- Source: bb

An attention-getter in the border. Attracts hummingbirds.

flowering tobacco

Nicotiana alata
'Nicki Red'
- Annual
- 1-3'
- Summer to fall
- Red

- Sun, part shade
- Sources: j, s, ff

Many flowers, which, unlike the white species, do not droop during the day. They are not fragrant. Long blooming. Good plant for beds, borders, or containers. Sow seed directly in the garden. Prefers rich, well-drained soil.

sweet alyssum

Lobularia maritima
'Wonderland Rose'
- Annual
- 3-4", spread to 10"
- Summer-frost
- Fragrant
- Rosy-purple
- Sun, part shade
- Sources: s, cc, dd

Good edging plant, warm-season groundcover, or "living mulch" in containers. Easy to grow from seed. Self-sows. White varieties most fragrant.

delphinium

Delphinium
'Blue Springs'
- Perennial
- 3-5'
- Late spring, early summer
- Blue

- Zones 2-7
- Sun
- Sources: gg, ii

Gorgeous, dramatic plants that require staking, especially against wind and heavy rain. Short-lived, so for continuous show, add several new plants each year.

daylily

Hemerocallis
'Happy Returns'
- Perennial
- 18"
- Early summer, reblooms
- Lemon yellow
- Zones 3-9
- Sun
- Sources: s, ee, ii

Reblooms in the north. Edible flowers. Grows best in good, well-drained soil. Divide every 3 to 5 years.

foxglove

Digitalis x mertonensis
- Perennial
- Late spring, summer
- Strawberry
- Zones 4-9
- Part shade, sun
- Sources: j, q, gg, ii

Impressive spikes with numerous 2-inch flowers. Easy to grow; prefers part shade. Grows best in rich, well-drained soil.

climbing rose

Rosa 'Blaze'
- Shrub
- 10'
- Late spring-frost
- Fragrant

- Red
- Zones 5-9
- Sun
- Sources: b, x

Great old variety with repeat bloom. Durable. Train to grow on a trellis, fence, pillar, or post. Disease resistant.

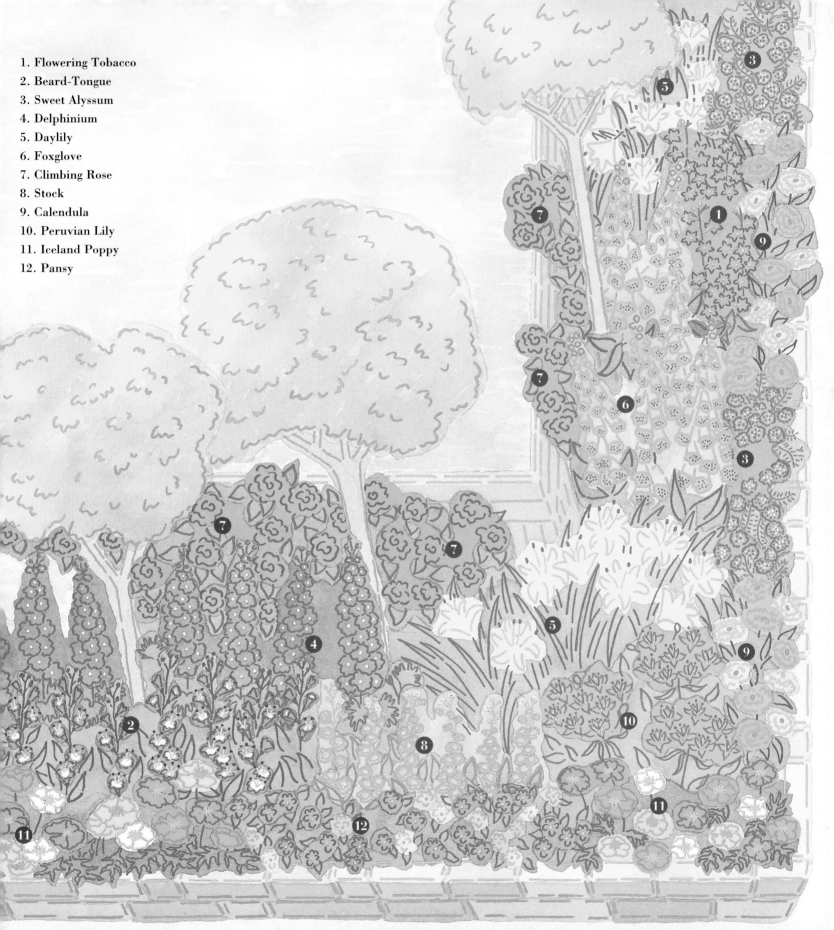

1. Flowering Tobacco
2. Beard-Tongue
3. Sweet Alyssum
4. Delphinium
5. Daylily
6. Foxglove
7. Climbing Rose
8. Stock
9. Calendula
10. Peruvian Lily
11. Iceland Poppy
12. Pansy

stock

Matthiola incana hyb.
- Biennial
- 18-30″
- Spring
- Fragrant
- White to purple
- Sun
- Sources: t, z

Grow as an annual; sow directly in the garden in early spring. Likes cool weather. Scented, even at night.

calendula

Calendula officinalis
'Art Shades'
- Annual
- 24"
- Summer to fall
- Apricot to cream
- Sun
- Source: dd

Many attractive varieties.
Versatile plant: ornamental,
dried, dye plant, and edible
flowers. Use petals as a saffron
substitute. Easy to grow.
Deadhead for continued bloom.

iceland poppy

Papaver nudicaule
- Perennial
- 1-3'
- Summer-fall
- Fragrant
- Yellow, white, orange, red
- Zones 7-10
- Sun
- Sources: g, r, cc

Bright, silky, fragrant, 1- to 3-
inch flowers. Short-lived; often
grown as an annual. Sow seeds
in fall or winter by scattering
on bare ground.

peruvian lily

Alstroemeria hyb.
- Perennial
- 2-4'
- Spring, summer
- Zones 6-10
- Sun
- Sources: n, dd, ii

Exotic-looking plant and
flowers. Blooms cut well and
are long lasting. Treat as a
tender bulb in colder areas; lift
and store indoors for winter.
Prefers rich, well-drained soil.
Mulch well.

pansy

Viola x *wittrockiana* hyb.
- Annual
- 6-9"
- Spring
- Mixed colors
- Part shade
- Sources: s, cc, dd

Charming additions to any
garden. Varieties in every color
of the rainbow. Edible flowers.
Start seed indoors 12 weeks
before spring frost-free date or
plant in fall. Prefers moist, rich
soil and cool weather.

enclosed
garden

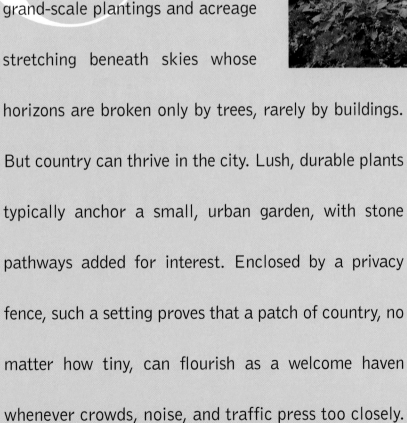

Country style can evoke images of grand-scale plantings and acreage stretching beneath skies whose horizons are broken only by trees, rarely by buildings. But country can thrive in the city. Lush, durable plants typically anchor a small, urban garden, with stone pathways added for interest. Enclosed by a privacy fence, such a setting proves that a patch of country, no matter how tiny, can flourish as a welcome haven whenever crowds, noise, and traffic press too closely.

Several surprises awaited Kristin and Craig Beddow as the spring thaw came soon after they moved into their south Minneapolis home. The deep Minnesota snow had covered a crumbling driveway (sprouting an assortment of weeds), a tumbling-down lattice fence in the back of the house, and, worst of all, a huge tree stump right in the center of the lawn. The challenges that faced Kristin and Craig did not daunt them, but careful planning was required to transform their small, 20 × 50-foot yard from an eyesore to an eye-catching garden.

The first major challenge was the tree stump, which Kristin did not remove. Instead, she decided to turn it into a focal point by mounding it with soil and creating a planting berm for perennials. This sunny spot is perfect for many types of daylilies, creeping thyme, sedum, and iris. Raised beds, like the planting berm, are ideal for any plant requiring good drainage; they're a great location for most silver-leafed plants, herbs, and scented geraniums.

Craig replaced the old, broken-down fence with a new cedar lattice fence and an arbor. He designed the fence to be tall enough to ensure some privacy, yet he wanted to avoid the closed-in feeling of a solid fence. The latticework lets in enough light and air for circulation. Clematis grows over the fence and arbor, adding shade, fragrance, and privacy.

The Beddows built a path from weather-smoothed stones found on their property. The path leads visitors around the berm and into the garden proper.

The large trees cast much shade. Many gardeners consider shade a drawback, thinking only about the sun-loving plants that they can't grow. Although sunflowers do not thrive in shade, many plants that make a strong visual impact in less than full sun. Kristin and Craig selected a number of reliable favorites for shade, including hosta, astilbe, bleeding heart, and ferns. However, they didn't incorporate ubiquitous varieties. Instead, they chose ones that had more visual interest. Variegated leaves with their lighter color patterns catch whatever light is available in the shade and reflect it. 'Golden Tiara' hosta, for example, with its chartreuse-edged leaves, is more noticeable than a plain, green-leafed hosta.

The Beddows' patience, persistence, and planning proved worthwhile. Their garden balances shade and sun.

FERNS FOR SHADE

Ferns provide long-season foliage interest and are among the most low-maintenance plants. Give ferns soil that's rich with organic material and plenty of moisture, and they'll prosper for years without further attention. Few plants, especially shade ones, are as carefree and beautiful.

Maidenhair ferns have a graceful semicircle of delicately textured leaves on wiry, black stems. In the garden, they gradually form a nice clump of foliage.

Other interesting ferns for shade include the Christmas fern, with individual leaves shaped like Christmas stockings, and Japanese painted fern with triolored, silvery-metallic fronds.

bringing order and beauty to chaos

Soften the formality of a brick walkway; let plants spill out of the beds. Opposite: Overview of the garden.

This neglected yard posed a challenge, not a problem.

That was the attitude Kristin and Craig Beddow of Minneapolis, Minnesota, took when faced with a new backyard that needed drastic improvement. Kristin, who has gardened her whole life, had early and very positive memories of visiting gardens with her mother. Creating order and beauty from this chaos was her goal. Kristin recalls that purple lilacs leaning against the house supplied the only color. She and Craig brought the yard to life with flowering plants. Today, leopard's plant, astilbe, rubrum lily, yarrow, high mallow, and other plants abound in their private garden.

male fern

Dryopteris filix-mas
- Perennial, fern
- 30"
- Foliage plant
- Green
- Zones 4-8
- Shade, part shade
- Sources: e, n, aa

Handsome with well-divided fronds; deciduous. Prefers neutral to acid soil, cool, moist woodlands.

astilbe

Astilbe x *arendsii*
- Perennial
- 18-48"
- Early-late summer
- White to red
- Zones 4-8

- Sun, part shade
- Sources: e, u, y, gg

Attractive, durable plant for shady spots. Fernlike foliage. Select hybrids by color or height requirements.

meadow rue

Thalictrum delavayi
- Perennial
- 3-5'
- Summer
- Pink, purple
- Zones 5-10
- Sun, part shade
- Sources: e, y, z, dd

Delicate, see-through look makes it perfect anywhere in the border—in front as a veil, or in back. Fern-like leaves; nicely floppy. Prefers rich soil. 'Hewitt's Double' is a good variety.

salvia

Salvia coccinea
'Lady in Red'
- Annual
- 12-18"
- Summer to fall
- Red
- Sun
- Sources: b, dd, ii

Great bedding plant; long-blooming flowers in tiers. Warmer shade of red than most salvias. Blooms early and long.

dwarf alberta spruce

Picea glauca 'Conica'
- Tree, evergreen
- 10-12' (in 30 years)
- Foliage plant
- Gray green needles
- Zones 2-6
- Sun
- Sources: e, y, bb

Very slow, dense growth; perfect conical shape. Nice accent plant in a mixed border or use as a miniature Christmas tree.

leopard plant

Ligularia x *hessei*
'Gregynog Gold'
- Perennial
- 5-6'
- Summer, late summer

- Orange-yellow
- Zones 4-10
- Part shade, sun
- Source: c

Big, leathery, dark-green leaves. Loose flower spikes have a relaxed feel. Grows best in moist, rich soil.

meadow phlox

Phlox maculata hyb.
- Perennial
- 1-3'
- Summer
- Fragrant
- Purple to white
- Zones 3-9
- Sun, part shade
- Sources: e, gg

Pretty flower clusters. Cut back for rebloom.

bird's nest spruce

Picea abies 'Nidiformis'
- Tree, evergreen
- 3-6' (in many years)
- Foliage plant
- Dark green
- Zones 2-7
- Sun
- Sources: e, y

Dwarf evergreen with a unique habit; dense, broad, and spreading with a flat top or nestlike depression in the center. Grows slowly.

silver thyme

Thymus vulgaris
'Argenteus'
- Perennial, herb
- 6-12"
- Summer
- Fragrant
- White
- Zones 5-9
- Sun
- Sources: f, v, y

Attractive, cream-edged leaves; culinary herb. Grows best in lean, well-drained soil.

sedum

Sedum kamtschaticum
- Perennial
- 12"
- Summer
- Yellow, turning crimson
- Zones 3-8
- Sun
- Sources: a, ff

Beautiful, mounding little plant. Current year stems bronze; old stems die. Requires well-drained, lean soil.

1. Male Fern
2. Meadow Rue
3. Astilbe
4. Salvia
5. Dwarf Alberta Spruce
6. Leopard Plant
7. Meadow Phlox
8. Bird's Nest Spruce
9. Silver Thyme
10. Sedum
11. Balloon Flower
12. Hosta
13. Gooseneck Loosestrife
14. Chrysanthemum
15. Cream Violet
16. Maidenhair Fern
17. Bellflower
18. Daylily
19. Rubrum Lily
20. Yarrow
21. New England Aster
22. Showy Stonecrop
23. Tickseed
24. Snow-in-Summer
25. Speedwell
26. Stonecrop
27. High Mallow
28. Regal Lily
29. Bleeding Heart
30. Foxglove
31. Clematis
32. Dead Nettle
33. Showy Stonecrop
34. Aster
35. Cranesbill

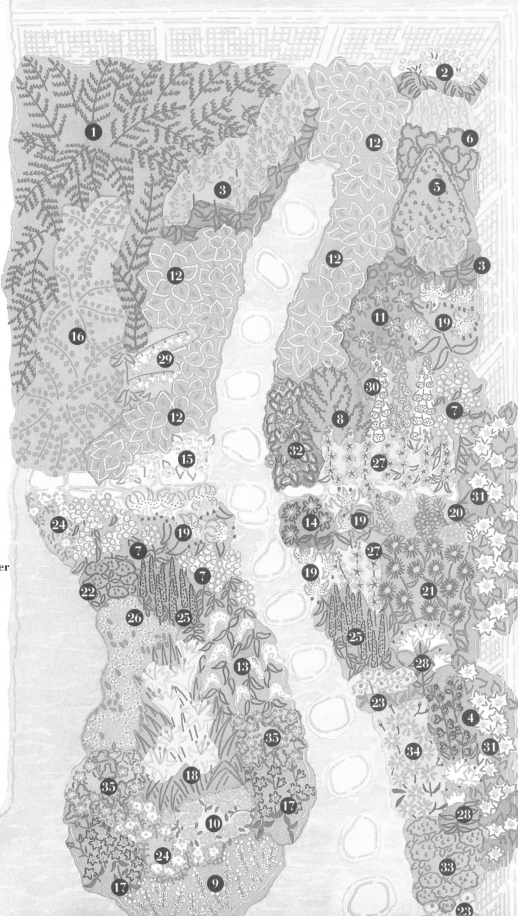

balloon flower

Platycodon grandiflorus
- Perennial
- 18-30″
- Summer
- Blue
- Zones 3-10
- Sun, part shade
- Sources: e, n, v, ii

Handsome, gray-green leaves grow in upright clumps. Long-blooming, cup-shaped flowers. Easy to grow.

gooseneck loosestrife

Lysimachia clethroides
- Perennial
- 30-36″
- Late summer
- White
- Zones 3-10
- Sun, part shade
- Sources: c, q, ii

Elegant, upright plant with arching flowers. Can be invasive in good soil; plant in nursery pot and plunge in ground.

hosta

Hosta 'Golden Tiara'
- Perennial
- 10-15″
- Late spring
- Light purple
- Zones 3-9
- Part shade, shade
- Sources: n, u, aa, ii

Nice, medium-green, heart-shaped leaves with irregular gold margins. Bold highlights for dark areas. Makes a good edging plant. Quickly forms clumps and can be divided.

chrysanthemum

Dendranthema x *grandiflorum* (*Chrysanthemum* x *moriflorum*) hyb.
- Perennial
- 1-6′
- Late summer to frost
- Yellow to red
- Zones 4-10
- Sun
- Sources: Buy locally

For a change, plant budded mums in spring. Don't pinch; they'll soon flower. Deadhead and they will rebloom in autumn.

cream violet

Viola striata
- Perennial
- 6-12"
- Early spring, spring
- White, cream white
- Zones 4-8
- Shade, part shade
- Source: hh

Unusual violet that's worth seeking out. Nice woodland plant with pale flowers striped with purple. Prefers rich, well-drained soil.

bellflower

Campanula portenschlagiana
- Perennial
- 6-9"
- Late spring, summer
- Blue, deep lavender
- Zones 5-10
- Sun, part shade
- Sources: e, y, dd, ii

Handsome, low mound of leaves covered with flowers. Vigorous plant. Excellent for the front of the border, planted in a rock wall, or in a container.

maidenhair fern

Adiantum pedatum
- Perennial
- Fern
- 18-24"
- Foliage plant
- Green foliage
- Zones 2-8
- Part shade, shade
- Sources: u, aa, ii

Delicate, lacy fans of fronds; black stems. Elegant woodland native in massed planting. Prefers rich, moist soil.

daylily

Hemerocallis 'Stella de Oro'
- Perennial
- 1-2'
- Early summer, repeats
- Yellow
- Zones 3-10
- Sun, part shade
- Sources: e, aa, ee, ii

Compact. Long-blooming with cheery yellow, edible flowers. Prefers rich, well-drained soils. Divide every 3 years.

rubrum lily

Lilium speciosum var.
rubrum
- Bulb, perennial
- 3-5'
- Summer
- Fragrant
- Rose
- Zones 3-10
- Sun
- Sources: d, ii

A classic; can have a
dozen 8-inch flowers per
stem. Good cut flower.

yarrow

Achillea millefolium
'Summer Pastels'
- Perennial
- 2'
- Summer
- Pink to orange pastels
- Zones 3-9
- Sun
- Sources: b, r, dd

Attractive fernlike
foliage; flat clusters of
flowers. Flowers good
cut fresh or dried.
Grows best in well-
drained soil. Will bloom
the first year when
grown from seed.

new england aster

Aster novae-angliae
'September Ruby'
- Perennial
- Fall to frost
- Rose pink

- Zones 4-9
- Sun
- Source: c

Bold color for the
autumn border. Will
naturalize. Good cut
flower. For showy,
bushy plants, pinch
early and frequently.

showy stonecrop

Hylotelephium
'Indian Chief'
- Perennial
- 2-3'
- Late spring, early fall
- Coppery-rose
- Zones 4-10
- Sun
- Sources: e, n

Coppery-rose flowers
change to brick red.
Attractive in winter.

tickseed

Coreopsis grandiflora
- Perennial
- 1-3'
- Early summer, summer
- Yellow
- Zones 5-10
- Sun, part shade
- Sources: e, gg

Many 2-inch, bright-
yellow flowers; long-
flowering. Extremely easy
to grow. Deadhead for
continuous flowering and
to keep plant tidy.

snow-in-summer

Cerastium tomentosum
- Perennial,
  groundcover
- 6-12"
- Late spring,
  early summer
- White
- Zones 3-10

- Sun
- Sources: Buy locally

Prostrate, aggressive
groundcover. Handsome
gray stems and leaves.
Requires full sun and
very well-drained soil.
Drought tolerant. Cut
back after it blooms.

speedwell

Veronica spicata hyb.
- Perennial
- 1-2'
- Summer
- Blue to red
- Zones 3-10
- Part shade
- Sources: b, z, dd

Dense plants covered
with little flowers on
tapering spikes. Easy-
to-grow, long-blooming
border plants.

stonecrop

Sedum acre 'Aureum'
- Perennial
- 3", spread 12"
- Summer
- Yellow
- Zones 4-8
- Sun
- Source: bb

Pale green mats
brighten in spring
with yellow new
growth. Noninvasive,
colorful accent for
stepping stones.
Drought tolerant.

high mallow

Malva sylvestris 'Zebrina'
(*Althea zebrina*)
- Perennial
- 3'
- Summer-fall
- White with purple
- Zones 3-9
- Sun
- Sources: b, s, dd, ii

Sturdy plant with striking, long-blooming flowers. Will tolerate a light frost. Short-lived plant, but will self-sow.

bleeding heart

Dicentra spectabilis 'Alba'
- Perennial
- 20"
- Spring, summer
- White
- Zones 4-10
- Part shade
- Sources: b, e, aa, dd, ii

Favorite garden plant; dissected foliage and arching stems of delicate white flowers. Dies back by midsummer.

regal lily

Lilium regale
- Bulb
- 4-6'
- Summer
- Fragrant
- White with rose buds
- Zones 3-9
- Sun
- Sources: dd, gg

Magnificent, large fragrant trumpets; up to 30 per plant. Needs staking. Comes back for many years. Grows well in average, well-drained soil.

foxglove

Digitalis purpurea
'Glittering Prizes'
- Biennial
- 4-6'
- Early summer
- White to purple
- Zones 4-8
- Part shade, sun
- Source: dd

Old garden favorite. Prefers rich, well-drained soil. Sow seed in August for bloom next year. Self-sows once it's established in the garden.

clematis

Clematis henryi (*Clematis* 'Henryi')
- Vine, perennial
- 5-8'
- Summer
- White
- Zones 6-10
- Part shade, sun
- Sources: e, g, s, gg

Flowers have brown accent; young foliage bronzed. Reblooms. Slow to establish in garden. Mulch well.

dead nettle

Lamium maculatum
'Chequers'
- Perennial, groundcover
- 8-12"
- Spring
- Mauve pink
- Zones 3-10
- Shade, part shade
- Source: e

Striking plant; green leaves with silver-accented midrib. Easy to grow, but may be invasive groundcover. Tolerates dry shade.

aster

Aster tataricus
- Perennial
- 6-8'
- Late summer-late fall
- Violet purple
- Zones 3-8
- Sun
- Sources: q, ii

Dramatic plant for fall. Needs lots of space. Completely covered with 1-inch flowers. Requires staking.

showy stonecrop

Hylotelephium (*Sedum*)
'Autumn Joy'
- Perennial
- 24-30"
- Late summer, early fall
- Pink to rose
- Zones 3-9
- Sun
- Sources: b, n, q, ii

Three-season interest. Let seed heads remain on plant in winter. Very easy to grow.

cranesbill

Geranium spp.
- Perennial
- 6-36"
- Late spring-early fall
- White to purple
- Zones 3-10
- Sun, part shade
- Sources: e, gg, ii

Forms mounds of attractive, durable foliage. Keep cutting off spent flowers to encourage rebloom. Long-blooming plant.

formal garden

Style, whether expressed in fashion, art, architecture, or gardening, is the hallmark of Italian culture. Here, it translates beautifully to this formal Virginian garden. The Italian flair for using statuary, fountains, pools, pillars, trellises, arbors, and shaded walkways amid lush greenery evolved over centuries. Flowers, in exquisite bursts of color, punctuate the verdant scene. Though allowed some freedom, nature is restrained by this gardener's artful hand.

The two contrasting shades of green draw the eye to a statue in the distance. *Opposite*: Trumpet vine.

eric E. Fitzpatrick, already an accomplished artist, traveled to Italy to study painting and sculpture and was captivated by the gardens he visited.

His fascination with the gardens stayed with him and turned him into a gardener. What Eric learned about classic garden elements and perspective he translated into his own Roanoke, Virginia, garden.

The Boboli Gardens, first begun during the Renaissance in the mid-16th century, impressed Eric with their awe-inspiring sculpture, fountains, pools, and plants. While walking around the gardens, Eric was impressed how the cool, trellised tunnels compelled him to follow the paths that eventually led to statues and fountains.

At Villa Lanta, Eric was inspired by a vantage point from which the entire garden was visible. At Isola Bella, an island in Lake Maggiore, Eric found a huge garden, divided into small sections. Here, the designer had ensured that all views were controlled—that is, only isolated sections rather than the whole could be seen.

Back home in Virginia, Eric worked on plans for his own garden, relying on vivid memories and sketches of the Italian gardens he had visited. However, he faced a challenge: His interpretation of a formal garden would have to fit into a modest 30 × 40-foot space.

Eric started by adding a tilt to the land, grading it upward from his studio to the back fence. This gradual rise allows him to see the entire pattern of the garden while he sits in his studio. From this vantage point, he also can view the lion's head rising up at the back of the pool.

The enclosed garden with ivy-covered arcades mimics Italian cloister courtyards. Dark-toned, high board fences, which seem to disappear from sight, back the trellis arches.

Lighting plays a dramatic role in Eric's garden. The lights, along with correct use of perspective, ornaments, architectural elements, and water, truly make this garden an Italian spectacle in America.

the influence of travel abroad

Raised Bed Illusions

All of the central beds are raised, as is the height of the trellises. This makes statues on either side of the garden closer to eye level. It also makes them seem larger.

Eric edged the beds with bricks placed on end and topped them with a horizontal layer. The bricks lean into the beds in order to keep additional soil (which was obtained from digging out the pool) in place.

It's easy to plant and maintain raised beds. In this garden they require little work, only replanting annuals and trimming the shrubs each spring. That means more time to daydream in a little piece of Italy.

A lion's head fountain drops water into a still, water lily studded pool. *Opposite:* Garden overview.

His garden takes this artist to **another place** when he gazes out the window of his Roanoke, Virginia, studio. With a single glance, Eric E. Fitzpatrick returns to the Italian countryside, away from the noise of nearby traffic and the pressures of work. The sound of water playing in his three fountains produces calming sensations and makes him forget he's near the Blue Ridge Mountains instead of his beloved Italian gardens. Eric's small, but elegant garden boasts formal elements such as planned perspective, low, clipped boxwood hedges, bed symmetry, and ponds and statuary functioning as central focal points.

trumpet vine

Campsis radicans
- Vine, woody
- To 40'
- Summer
- Scarlet-orange
- Zones 4-9
- Sun, part shade
- Sources: a, j, y, dd

Vibrant flowers attract hummingbirds. Blooms on new wood. Grows in poor, dry soil. Makes suckers; aggressive vine.

cattail

Typha latifolia
- Perennial
- 3-9'
- Summer
- Brown spike
- Zones 3-10
- Sun
- Sources: m, n

Striking water/bog plant. Use giant and thick cattails for larger ponds or bogs, miniature cattails for small tubs. Redwing blackbirds use cattails for nesting material.

small-leafed holly

Ilex crenata 'Convexa'
- Shrub, evergreen
- 7-9', spread to 24'
- Foliage plant
- Green
- Zones 5-8

- Sun, part shade
- Sources: e, g, n

Dense, attractive, evergreen shrub with small, dark green leaves. May be pruned and shaped. Makes a good hedge, whether pruned or left natural.

lavender cotton

Santolina chamaecyparissus & *S. rosmarinifolia*
- Perennial
- 2', spread to 4'
- Summer
- Fragrant
- Yellow
- Zones 6-9
- Sun
- Sources: e, f, n, v, z

Aromatic leaves. Prefers lean, sandy, dry soil. Prune after flowering. Drought tolerant.

purple basil

Ocimum basilicum 'Purple Ruffles'
- Annual, herb
- 18-24"
- Summer-fall
- Fragrant
- Pale pink
- Sun
- Sources: b, s, t

Attractive, large, ruffled, deep purple leaves are edible. Perfect bedding plant, in borders, herb garden, or containers. Flowers are somewhat insignificant, but edible.

korean boxwood

Buxus microphylla var. *koreana*
- Shrub, evergreen
- 24-30", spread to 5'
- Green foliage

- Zones 4-9
- Sun, part shade
- Sources: a, e, v

Slow-growing, deep-rooted, evergreen. Mulch with leaf mold to keep roots cool. Protect from drying winds.

hardy water lily

Nymphaea 'Charles de Meurville'
- Perennial
- 6", spread to 28"
- Summer
- Deep claret with white
- Zones 3-10
- Sun
- Source: m

Magnificent, large flowers; glossy-green floating leaves. Grow in pots in at least 18" of water.

signet marigold

Tagetes tenuifolia
Gem Hybrids
- Annual
- 6-9″
- Summer-fall
- Fragrant
- Yellow or tangerine
- Sun
- Sources: b, f, v, z, cc

Fern-like foliage with citrusy tarragon aroma. Good for containers or herb garden.

grape

Vitis vinifera
- Vine, woody
- 50′, pruned to 12-20′
- Fall fruit
- Fruit: green, red, black
- Zones 7-10
- Sun
- Sources: b, p, s

Handsome, large-leafed vine. Needs special pruning for harvestable fruit. Vines need support and training. Requires deeply cultivated, rich, well-drained soil.

french lavender

Lavandula dentata
- Perennial, herb
- 18-30″
- Summer-fall
- Fragrant
- Purple
- Zones 9-10
- Sun
- Sources: f, v, jj

Attractive, aromatic gray-green leaves with indented edges. Can be trained as a topiary.

impatiens

Impatiens 'Tango'
- Annual
- 18-24″
- Early summer-fall
- Orange
- Part shade, sun
- Sources: s, dd

All-American Award winner. Unusual leaves with bronze-green variegations. Easy to grow; long-blooming. Likes warm weather. Takes more sun than most impatiens.

cottage
garden

apristine setting can inspire individuals to retreat and to contemplate nature, their relationship with it, and ultimately their own way of being. Henry David Thoreau's sojourn at Walden Pond became a journey of self-discovery. He found life rich if he kept it simple. On a rugged, tree-covered hilltop in western Maine, two gardeners, as did Thoreau, learned to balance nature, company, and solitude.

Use landscape elements, such as stones and tree trunks, for their textural quality. *Opposite:* Tickseed.

Garden overview—
lilies dominate this
border, towering
over other plants.

b

uried in the overgrown thicket of poplar and ash trees, fragrant, mature lilacs and ancient gnarled Baldwin apple trees grew in a Maine orchard at least a century old. Homeowners Carolyn and David Jenson surveyed the scene and decided to homestead.

Carolyn slowly reclaimed the land, while David began work on the new, shingled cottage. The couple retained old specimens of maple, birch, white pine, and poplar to serve as a framework for the garden. So many large stumps remained, some a foot or more in diameter and less than a foot apart, that they couldn't be dug out. The Jensons cut them as close to the ground as possible, then dealt with the stumps by "sod-top gardening," an inventive solution to the problem.

Carolyn covered the stumps with layers of wet newspaper, rotting hay, and about 6 inches of well-composted horse dressing (manure mixed with wood chips). These "raised beds" were ready for immediate planting. This mixture, with generous quantities of natural forest loam, more horse dressing, and a sprinkling of lime added each year, provides nutrition for a wide variety of old-fashioned country flowers, such as lilies, pansies, and corydalis. Carolyn also planted large specimens of Pacific Giant hybrid delphiniums in every shade of blue, a lovely complement to the clear Maine sky.

A surprisingly varied range of plants survive, adapt, and thrive in this environment covering zones 3 to 4. Miniature dicentra naturalize, showing their cheery pink and white happy faces each spring. In fact, Carolyn has made naturalized landscaping a primary goal. Bulbs multiply and flowers self-sow, resulting in serendipitous compositions. Mallows self-sow and are allowed to remain in the vegetable garden or among the raspberries (a must-have small fruit for a country garden).

Carolyn experiments with designs, such as island beds and vine bowers, using traditional garden perennials in new ways. She cuts the flowers for fresh arrangements or dries them to use in decorative projects.

The Jensons' hard work and creativity bring rich rewards. Their cottage garden offers fresh-cut flowers by the armload and reminds the couple daily of the satisfaction gained from restoring an old homestead to its original beauty.

No Longer Gardening In Solitude

The Jensons developed their property and home in solitude, thinking no one even knew they lived there. Then one day the garden club showed up, inquiring about the gardens.

Now Carolyn has a business, Maine Cottage Gardens, and stays busy conducting gardening workshops, marketing fresh-cut and dried flowers, and creating pressed flower arrangements. The Jensons ended up in Maine by chance, not unlike many of their flowers which bloom where the seeds land.

a reclaimed garden

Reclaiming a **rustic** house and garden changed the lives

of David and Carolyn Pettengill Jenson, who moved to the mountains of western Maine after an unsuccessful business venture in Seattle. They restored a cabin, actually a secluded hunting lodge without electricity or running water, on the family's 19th-century farm. Despite minimal comforts, the Jensons enjoyed the privacy and the opportunity to get in touch with "being country folk." Creating a garden was their first connection to the land. As their garden and business flourished, so did their attachment to their new homestead and lifestyle.

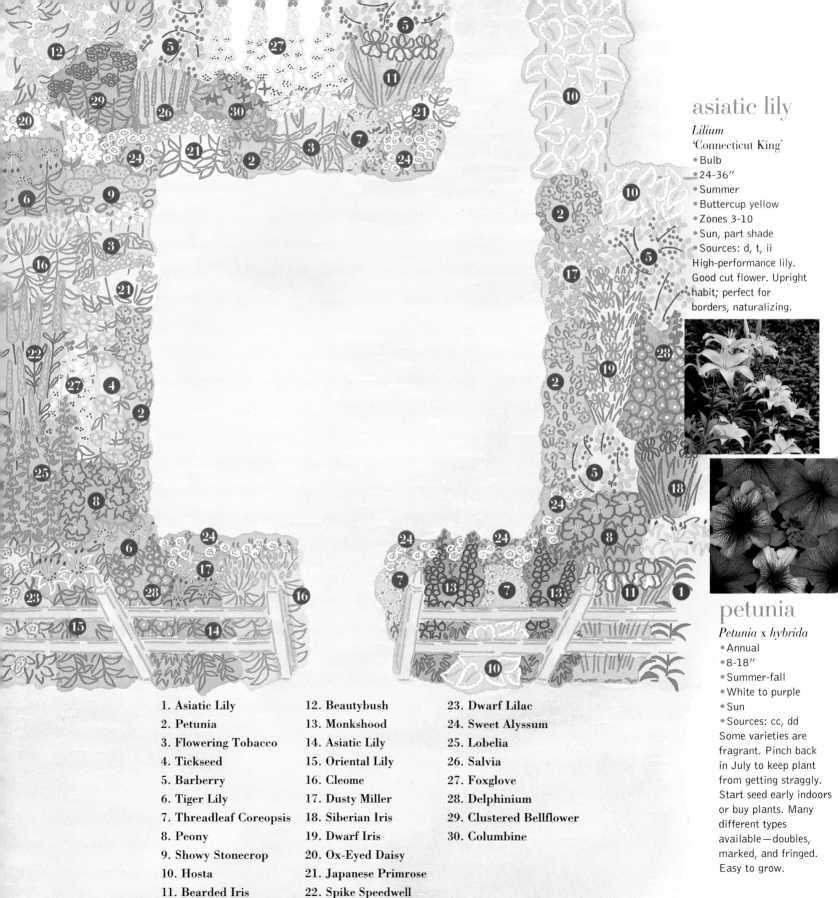

asiatic lily

Lilium
'Connecticut King'
- Bulb
- 24-36"
- Summer
- Buttercup yellow
- Zones 3-10
- Sun, part shade
- Sources: d, t, ii

High-performance lily. Good cut flower. Upright habit; perfect for borders, naturalizing.

petunia

Petunia x *hybrida*
- Annual
- 8-18"
- Summer-fall
- White to purple
- Sun
- Sources: cc, dd

Some varieties are fragrant. Pinch back in July to keep plant from getting straggly. Start seed early indoors or buy plants. Many different types available—doubles, marked, and fringed. Easy to grow.

1. Asiatic Lily
2. Petunia
3. Flowering Tobacco
4. Tickseed
5. Barberry
6. Tiger Lily
7. Threadleaf Coreopsis
8. Peony
9. Showy Stonecrop
10. Hosta
11. Bearded Iris
12. Beautybush
13. Monkshood
14. Asiatic Lily
15. Oriental Lily
16. Cleome
17. Dusty Miller
18. Siberian Iris
19. Dwarf Iris
20. Ox-Eyed Daisy
21. Japanese Primrose
22. Spike Speedwell
23. Dwarf Lilac
24. Sweet Alyssum
25. Lobelia
26. Salvia
27. Foxglove
28. Delphinium
29. Clustered Bellflower
30. Columbine

flowering tobacco

Nicotiana sylvestris
- Perennial, tender
- 4-6'
- Summer-fall
- Fragrant
- White
- Zones 8-10
- Sun, part shade
- Sources: r, s, z, dd

Night-fragrant flowers. Treat as an annual in colder areas. Self-sows.

tickseed

Coreopsis grandiflora 'Early Sunrise'
- Perennial
- 2'
- Summer–fall
- Golden-yellow
- Zones 3-9
- Sun
- Sources: c, y, ii

Lovely, semidouble flowers on a neat, compact plant. Very long-blooming. Deadhead for neatness and for ongoing bloom.

barberry

Berberis thunbergii 'Aurea'
- Shrub
- 3-4'
- Foliage
- Yellow, yellow/green
- Zones 4-10

- Sun
- Sources: a, e, g, n, y

This is a great plant to provide contrast in the garden. Its yellow leaves (yellow/green in shade) sparkle against deeper hued barberries. Slow growing. Deciduous.

tiger lily

Lilium lancifolium (*Lilium tigrinum*)
- Bulb, perennial
- 3-4'
- Late summer, early fall
- Orange with black spots
- Zones 3-10
- Sun
- Source: ii

Naturalizes well. Easy to grow. Don't plant near other lilies.

threadleaf coreopsis

Coreopsis verticillata 'Moonbeam'
- Perennial
- 2'
- Summer, fall
- Pale yellow
- Zones 3-10
- Sun
- Sources: e, g, q, y, ii

Attractive, fernlike foliage; cheery flowers. One of the longest-blooming perennials. Very drought-tolerant.

peony

Paeonia lactiflora 'Bright Knight'
- Perennial
- 30"
- Late spring
- Fragrant
- Deep rose pink
- Zones 2-10
- Sun
- Source: l

Upright clumps of nice, green, strong stemmed foliage. Single flowers with bright yellow center. Highly perfumed. Prefer deep, rich soil. Needs support.

showy stonecrop

Hylotelephium (*Sedum*) 'Autumn Joy'
- Perennial
- 24-30"
- Late summer, early fall
- Pink to rose
- Zones 3-9
- Sun,
- Sources: b, n, q, ii

Neat, succulent foliage. Multiseason interest. Long-lasting blooms.

hosta

Hosta undulata var. *albo-marginata*
- Perennial
- 12"
- Late summer
- Fragrant
- Purple
- Zones 3-9
- Part shade, shade
- Sources: b, aa

Fragrant spikes of flowers rise 24 inches above the handsomely variegated foliage. Great in mass plantings or used as a groundcover.

bearded iris

Iris germanica hyb.
- Perennial
- 16-30"
- Spring, early summer
- White to purple
- Zones 3-10
- Sun
- Sources: n, ii

Elegant flowers; good for cutting. Easy to grow in very well-drained soil. Plant rhizome flat with top third to one-half above soil level.

monkshood

Aconitum napellus
- Perennial
- 3'
- Summer, late summer
- Blue
- Zones 2-9
- Sources: v, dd

Good looking plant with leafy stems and helmet-shaped flowers. Cut back after flowering to encourage a second bloom. Poisonous.

beautybush

Kolkwitzia amabilis
- Shrub
- Early spring
- 6-10'
- Pink
- Zones 4-8
- Sun
- Sources: e, g, dd, gg

Pretty flowering shrub with an upright, vase shape. Not to be confused with beautyberry; this one doesn't have decorative berries. May rebloom sporadically in fall.

asiatic lily

Lilium 'Corina'
- Bulb
- 30-36"
- Early summer
- Scarlet
- Zones 3-10
- Sun, part shade
- Sources: d, s, ii

Luminous red flowers with maroon spots near throat. Plant where it can catch the early morning or late afternoon light. Good cut flower. Naturalizes.

oriental lily

Lilium 'Imperial Pink'
- Bulb
- 3-4'
- Summer
- Fragrant
- Pink, edged white
- Zones 3-10
- Sun, part shade
- Sources: d, s, ii

Magnificent flowers. Excellent cut flower (remove stamens to avoid pollen stains). Prefers well-drained, good garden soil.

dusty miller

Senecio cineraria hyb.
- Biennial
- 18-30"
- Yellow
- Silvery-gray
- Zones 4-10
- Sun
- Sources: b, t, dd

Biennial usually grown as an annual. If it overwinters, it will bloom the second year. However, it's grown mainly as a foliage plant for its lovely silvery leaves and stems.

cleome

Cleome hassleriana hyb.
- Annual
- 3-4'
- Summer to fall
- White to violet
- Sun, part shade
- Sources: b, s, t, dd

Also called spider flower and spider plant. Showy clusters of flowers with very prominent stamens. Prickly stems. Sow seed when soil warms in spring; thin seedlings. Easy to grow; self-sows.

siberian iris

Iris sibirica
- Perennial
- 2-4'
- Late spring, early summer
- Purple to white
- Zones 4-10
- Part shade/sun
- Sources: j, q, y

Flowers top stately, upright foliage. Handsome cut flowers. Wide range of hues; some blooms velvety. Prefers rich, well-drained soil.

dwarf iris

Iris cristata
- Perennial
- 6-10"
- Spring
- Lilac to purple
- Zones 6-9
- Sun, part shade
- Sources: q, aa, hh

Elegant fans of sword-shaped leaves. Dainty groundcover for part shade. Prefers rich soil.

ox-eyed daisy

Leucanthemum vulgare
(*Chrysanthemum leucanthemum*)
- Perennial
- 24"
- Early summer
- White
- Zones 3-10
- Sun
- Sources: j, v, z

Best-loved daisy with cheery flowers. Good for naturalized areas and meadows. Spreads and will self-sow. Easy to grow. Named varieties available.

japanese primrose

Primula japonica
- Perennial
- 30"
- Late spring, early summer
- White to red
- Zones 5-9

- Part shade, shade
- Sources: e, hh, ii

Easiest primrose for moist, damp spots. When it's happy in its surroundings it'll self-sow and become a large patch. Requires rich soil.

spike speedwell

Veronica spicata
'Heidekind'
- Perennial
- 18-24"
- Summer
- Wine red
- Zones 4-10
- Sun, part shade
- Source: y

Compact plant with many long-blooming flower spikes.

dwarf lilac

Syringa patula
'Miss Kim'
- Shrub
- 3-5'
- Spring
- Fragrant
- Lilac
- Zones 3-8
- Sun
- Sources: a, e, gg

Small-growing lilac that's good for mass planting or mixed borders. Good fall color.

sweet alyssum

Lobularia maritima
- Annual
- 3-4", spread to 10"
- Summer-frost
- Fragrant
- White
- Sources: b, k, t, dd

Clusters of small, white, honey-scented flowers make this a beautiful edging plant in a bed, or in a container as a living mulch. Easy to grow from seed. Self-sows, especially in warm winter areas.

lobelia

Lobelia siphilitica
'Safire Pink'
- Perennial
- 2-3'
- Late summer - early fall
- Pink
- Zones 4-9
- Sun
- Sources: c, f, v, aa

Stately plant with vertical, stiff stems. Good cut flowers. Prefers rich, moist soil.

salvia

Salvia 'East Friesland'
- Perennial
- 18-24"
- Summer, fall
- Purple
- Zones 5-10
- Sun
- Sources: c, e, o, s

Handsome gray-green foliage on erect stems. Clump forming. Fertilize monthly during growing season. Deadhead for continuous bloom. Divide every 3 years.

foxglove

Digitalis grandiflora
- Perennial
- 24-30"
- Late spring, summer
- Creamy yellow
- Zones 3-10
- Sun, part shade
- Sources: j, q, v

An underutilized foxglove with unique curving flower stem. Blends well with light and dark colored flowers. Prefers rich, well-drained soil.

clustered bellflower

Campanula glomerata 'Superba'
- Perennial
- 2-3'
- Early summer
- Violet-blue
- Zones 4-8
- Sun, part shade
- Sources: e, g, aa

Big upward-facing flower clusters on erect stems. Needs good, well-drained soil.

delphinium

Delphinium elatum Pacific Hybrids
- Perennial
- 3-8'
- White to blue
- Summer
- Zones 3-10
- Sun
- Sources: b, k, r, t

Clumps of elegant, dramatic flowers. Plants are short-lived, add new plants into the garden every two years to maintain a mass planting. Prefers rich soil.

columbine

Aquilegia alpina
- Perennial
- 12-24"
- Early summer, summer
- Blue
- Zones 3-10
- Sun, part shade
- Sources: j, v, aa

Nicely divided, ferny leaves; long-blooming; nodding flowers. Grows best in part shade with well-drained soil.

pocket

garden

Old wheelbarrows make excellent planters. Make sure they have drainage holes. *Opposite*: Foxglove.

*a*lways intriguing, pocket gardens give the old adage "great things come in small packages" fresh meaning. This plot, tucked neatly on property first settled more than 200 years ago in Newport, Rhode Island, is the handiwork of its free-spirited owners. Vintage and antique folk art pops up among herbs and perennials that flourish freely. The garden is all the more charming because its shape actually resembles a pocket ... so many delights in such a cunning space.

in the heart of Newport, Rhode Island, blooms the small, quaint garden of Lynn and Maurice de la Valetta, a showcase of plants mingled with folk art.

the de la Valettas. A grape arbor, covered and shaded by entwined rugosa roses and Concord grapevines, became an outdoor room and natural extension from the house. Memories of visits to Italy and the south of France inspired their grape arbor, which now functions as their outdoor breakfast room.

this tiny pocket garden. The de la Valettas' love of primitive wood carvings spills over into their garden's decor. Often, they place gallery items amid the flowers and herbs.

perennials and herbs, with "useful" plants. Currently, raspberries form one border, while parsley makes up another. One year, the couple edged their beds with Bibb lettuce.

They love herbs, so a bed of chives, oregano, and basil grows within easy reach. Mint is

PERSONAL STYLE IN THE GARDEN
The artistic inclinations of the de la Valettas helped guide them in their choice of garden decor. Their love of rustic objects influenced their choice of garden design and furnishings.

a folk art paradise realized

These gallery owners and gardeners created a space that seems spontaneous and unplanned. To achieve this look, they had to make the garden appear more spacious than it was. So the de la Valettas expanded it in one surprising direction—up. Incorporating trelliswork and arbors into the design gave the garden height.

Then they played up rustic charm. A local craftsman made the trelliswork out of split cedar to achieve the gnarled look desired by

The de la Valettas use old wood to add character to their garden. Vintage wooden boxes serve as planters, and buff-colored jars hold blowsy flower arrangements—for indoors and out. Seedlings grow out of old boxes discarded by a shoelace factory. Aged and weathered furniture, such as a worn wooden chair and table, contributes to the relaxed country look in

Vintage bricks form shaded, V-shaped paths. Their varying sizes and uneven placement enhance the roughly textured setting.

The de la Valettas, never staid, enjoy changing their plants. They like to edge their plot, full of colorful

planted in a large tub to control its wandering ways.

Mixing flowers and herbs contributes to the garden's informal mood. Despite its size and rather funky facade, the de la Valettas' garden makes a bold, arty statement.

You can achieve a similar country look by searching for old wooden chairs, small tables, or plant stands. To protect wood objects, use a wood sealer.

Accessorize your outdoor rooms as you would indoor rooms—in your own personal style. For example, adding lace tablecloths and other vintage linens to outdoor furniture instantly changes the whole look and feeling of a garden.

Simple items, such as a pillow and hat, personalize a garden space. *Opposite*: Overview of the garden.

These art dealers desired a fun, spirited garden, where they could show off their latest folk objects and good-looking perennials, and still reap a harvest of wonderful herbs and vegetables. The de la Valettas' wish was rather ambitious , considering their backyard measured no more than 100 × 25 feet Interestingly, when they started work, their colonial-era townhouse with a former stable was only a weekend place. Now, because of a unique garden plan, it's their personal paradise where watering cans, bird houses, urns, vintage planters, and other collectibles provide almost as much ornamentation as the plants themselves.

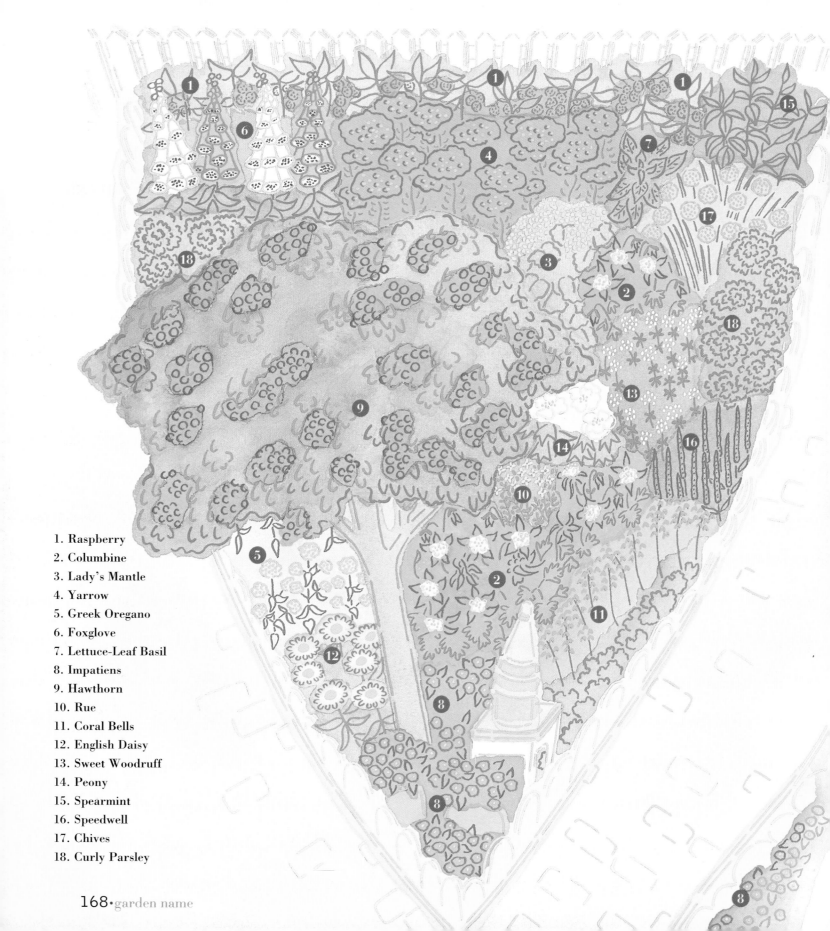

1. Raspberry
2. Columbine
3. Lady's Mantle
4. Yarrow
5. Greek Oregano
6. Foxglove
7. Lettuce-Leaf Basil
8. Impatiens
9. Hawthorn
10. Rue
11. Coral Bells
12. English Daisy
13. Sweet Woodruff
14. Peony
15. Spearmint
16. Speedwell
17. Chives
18. Curly Parsley

columbine

Aquilegia canadensis
- Perennial
- 12-24"
- Late spring, early summer
- White to red, bicolor
- Zones 3-10
- Sun
- Sources: j, q, y

Decorative ferny-leaves. Grows best in well-drained soil. Tough plant. Self-sows.

raspberry

Rubus idaeus 'Heritage'
- Shrub
- 6'
- Summer,
- Fruit, red
- Zones 5-9
- Sun

- Sources: p, t

Wonderful fruit, best picked in the morning. Plant in 12-inch wide strips. Requires support. Cut down to ground level in spring.

lady's mantle

Alchemilla mollis
- Perennial
- 1-2'
- Late spring, early summer
- Chartreuse
- Zones 3-9
- Sun
- Sources: t, y, aa, ii

Ornamental, scalloped, gray-green leaves are exquisite in the morning with a drop of dew on them. Chartreuse flowers are good cut fresh or dried.

yarrow

Achillea millefolium 'Paprika'
- Perennial
- 2'
- Summer
- Sunset red with yellow
- Zones 2-9
- Sun
- Source: e

Flat clusters of spicy-red blooms. Flowers are good cut fresh or dried. When flowers begin to fade, cut stems back halfway to encourage rebloom in late summer or early fall. Prefers well-drained soil. Will flower the first year when grown from seed.

greek oregano

Origanum heracleoticum (*Origanum virens*)
- Perennial, herb
- 1-2'
- Summer to fall
- Fragrant
- Pale pink
- Zones 7-10
- Sun
- Source: f

Best oregano; aromatic leaves and flowers. Needs well-drained soil.

foxglove

Digitalis purpurea 'Glittering Prizes'
- Biennial
- 4-6'
- Early summer
- White to purple, spotted
- Zones 4-8
- Part shade, sun
- Source: dd

Old garden favorite. Sow seed in August for bloom next year. Self-sows, so it seems like it's perennial. Requires rich, well-drained soil.

lettuce-leaf basil

Ocinum basilicum 'Basilico Monstruosa'
- Annual, herb
- 1-3'
- Fragrant
- Summer to frost
- White

- Sun
- Sources: f, t, v

Culinary herb, with an assertive licorice flavor. Easy to grow from seed. Pinch and use leaves; flavor gets very strong when plant flowers.

hawthorn

Crataegus monogyna
- Tree
- 20-30'
- Spring
- Fragrant
- White
- Zones 4-7
- Sun
- Source: e

Multiseason interest. Sweetly scented blooms. Shiny green leaves. Bright red fall fruit.

impatiens

Impatiens walleriana hyb.
- Annual
- 12-24"
- Summer-frost
- White to purple
- Part shade, shade

- Source: t

Extremely easy-to-grow, colorful plants. Non-stop flowering in shade; provides quick color for tough spots. Prefers moist soil.

rue

Ruta graveolens
- Perennial, herb
- 1-3'
- Late spring, summer
- Chartreuse
- Zones 4-9
- Sun
- Sources: j, s, t, v

Decorative herb (not culinary). Grown as a foliage plant for its handsome blue-green leaves. Airy chartreuse yellow flowers. Many people get contact dermatitis from touching the plant.

coral bells

Heuchera sanguinea 'Brandon Pink'
- Perennial
- 12-18"
- Spring, summer
- Pink
- Zones 3-10
- Sun

- Source: c

Durable, good looking plant for the front of the border. Flowers are airy, veillike—can see through them even though they rise well above the leaves. Prefers rich, well-drained soil.

sweet woodruff

Galium odoratum
- Perennial, herb
- 6-8"
- Late spring
- White
- Zones 5-9
- Shade, part shade
- Sources: j, s, v, aa

Nice groundcover herb for shady, moist areas. Dried leaves have vanilla, haylike scent. Use fresh in May wine and dried in potpourri.

english daisy

Bellis perennis
- Perennial
- 6-8"
- Late spring, early summer
- White-to-red
- Zones 3-10
- Sun, part shade
- Source: s

Dainty but sturdy plant for interplanting with spring-blooming bulbs or as edging. Many hues, singles, and semidoubles.

peony

Paeonia lactiflora 'Moonrise'
- Perennial
- 2-3'
- Spring
- Fragrant

- Creamy white with yellow
- Zones 2-10
- Source: l

Spectacular garden favorite. Handsome foliage good for arrangements. Needs deep, rich soil.

spearmint

Mentha spicata
- Perennial, herb
- 2'
- Summer
- Fragrant
- Zones 3-10
- Sun, part shade
- Sources: b, r, v, cc

Aromatic, edible; aggressive groundcover. To keep from running rampant, mow when blooming; or plant in nursery pot and plunge in the ground.

chives

Allium schoenoprasum
- Bulb, herb
- 18"
- Early summer
- Blue-purple
- Zones 3-10
- Sun
- Sources: s, t, v, cc

Ornamental and edible grasslike leaves and pompon flowers. Usually grown as a perennial. Cut back after flowering. Good container plant.

speedwell

Veronica austriaca
'Crater Lake Blue'
- Perennial
- 12"
- Late spring, summer
- Gentian blue
- Zones 3-10
- Sun, part shade
- Sources: e, dd, ii

One of the best-blue flowers for the summer garden. Cut back after flowering to encourage rebloom. May need light brush-staking.

curly parsley

Petroselinum crispum
- Biennial, herb
- 18"
- Foliage herb
- Green
- Sun, part shade
- Sources: f, r, v

Attractive, underutilized edible with curly leaves. Beautiful edging plant. Usually grown as an annual. Tolerant of cold and some frost. Soak seed overnight before planting.

creating
your
country
garden

gazebos, paths, gates, picket fences, lush plantings, and garden ornaments—are just some of the elements you can use to make a country garden. You've seen examples of some of the best gardens from across America. Now it's time to transform your own piece of land into a little bit of country. Choose one of the preceding plans and follow the steps outlined in the forthcoming pages. Before you know it, you'll be relaxing on a comfortable chair, with a bouquet of flowers from your garden.

Getting Started

How you and your family spend your time has a major impact on what your landscape and garden will look like. Answer the following questions to determine how best to use your outdoor space. Do you want to have family gatherings and/or wish to minimize time working on your lawn? Are you just starting to get your hands dirty, or is gardening a passion? Do you have a special interest in vegetables, cut flowers, herbs, water gardening, fragrant plants, or wildlife?

Your climate and location will determine what kinds of plants you need to surround your home. In warm areas, you'll want deciduous

In a suburban yard, the garden edges the lawn. Flat stones act as a mowing strip.

creating a country style of your own

barbecues on your patio or deck? Do the kids need space to play a lively game of touch football, or do you want space for a more genteel game of croquet? Do you hate mowing and

trees to shade the house or patio, especially during hot summer months. If you live on the coast, you'll probably grow a windbreak of salt-tolerant plants.

A lush country garden in a rural setting adjoins a meadow.

Understanding Your Property

You need to understand the growing conditions of your property. Find out what type(s) of soil (sand, clay, loam, etc.) you have. If you haven't done so in the past two years, have the soil pH checked.

Determine how much sun and what the shade patterns are for the area you'll be gardening. Remember that deciduous trees lose their leaves and that

the angle of the sun changes throughout the year, so the amount of sun and shade changes with the seasons.

Check whether you have any particularly wet spots or very dry areas. Determine the direction of prevailing winds.

It's important to know your hardiness zone (see USDA hardiness zone map on *page 177*). This will help you select the plants that are best suited to your winter conditions.

Plan on Paper

Before you start planting, draw an overall landscape plan on paper. Make it to scale and include everything on your property—the house, all

existing structures, decks, driveways, and walkways. It's not hard to do using a copy of your property survey and graph paper.

Now, draw in all the beds, borders, and plants you want. Although it seems like a lot of work, it's much easier to move plants and pathways on paper.

Keep the plans in a 3-ring binder with pockets. Use it to store before and after pictures, notes about plants, and future plans.

Know What You Want

Most gardeners' desires know no bounds, but their resources—time, money, and space—are limited. To help decide what's really important, make a list of everything you want to have in the garden—not just plants. Include items such as a pond, trellis, brick path, or gazing ball—anything that says country garden to you. From that list, choose your top 10 items. Then narrow it down to the five most important. No matter what else goes into the garden, be sure you incorporate those five, and you'll be happy with your creation.

Start Small, Be Bold

Start with a single small project—a bed or border. Large-scale plans can be executed over a long time frame. By doing small projects, you get satisfaction from completing them, gain new skills, learn how much time gardening takes, and see how it fits into your life.

Don't worry—every gardener makes mistakes, learns from them, and even laughs at them later on. If a plant dies, dig it up and put it on the compost pile. In time, it will feed other plants. If a plant doesn't do well in one place—move it. It's all part of the process.

A rustic wheelbarrow serves as a focal point in this country garden.

And, be bold. It's your garden, and in the end, you're the only one it has to please. So grow whatever you want, whether it's giant pumpkins, orange flowers, or lavenders— go ahead. Do it and then enjoy the garden.

Design Choices

There's no limit to what your garden can be. Visit public, private, and botanic gardens for ideas. Take photos, make lists, or sketch plant combinations so you can refresh your memory later. Think about what you really love and incorporate that in your garden.

Use all or part of one of the plans in this book to inspire your garden. Certainly, it will not end up looking exactly the same, but it will be beautiful and satisfying.

Types of Gardens

There are many types of gardens to consider, depending on your location and needs.

An island bed is an irregularly shaped area cut out of the middle of the lawn and filled with an assortment of plants. A mixed border includes all types of plants in the same area—trees, shrubs, perennials, and annuals. A cutting garden contains flowering plants to cut for bouquets and arrangements.

You also may choose to specialize or have an area for roses, herbs, vegetables, bulbs, succulents, or anything else you like. Nature may dictate your choice. For example, a shady area would require growing plants that thrive with less than six

hours of sunlight.

If you love flowers that perfume the air or leaves which are aromatic when touched, grow a scented garden.

Water gardens are becoming ever more popular with the advent of flexible liners. A water garden can be as simple as a tub with a couple of fish and a water lily or as elaborate as a pond with a stream and waterfalls.

You may want to grow a garden that attracts birds or butterflies: Select plants for shelter and food, and be sure to include a water feature—even a small birdbath will do.

Nurture Your Soil

The key to your garden's success is the quality of the soil. Soil anchors every plant, while supplying most of its nutritional needs. Unless you're building a rock garden or water garden, the best thing you can do for your

plants is to incorporate organic matter into the soil. Peat moss, leaf mold, manure, and compost improve sandy or clay soil.

Compost for Goodness

Composting is simple—pile layers of vegetable waste, grass clippings, and leaves in a sunny location and let them rot. Alternate layers of brown and green ingredients; leave a depression in the center of the pile. Keep the pile moist and in a year or so, you'll have rich, dark compost—

gardeners' black gold. Turning the pile occasionally speeds up the process.

If you don't want to build a pile, just bury small amounts of grass clippings or vegetable waste directly in your garden, where it will break down over time.

You can compost lots of kitchen and garden items—coffee grounds, eggshells, fruit and vegetable scraps, grass clippings, flowers, leaves (shred oak leaves as they're slow to break down), farm animal manure, shredded newspaper (black and white only), plant clippings, sawdust, soil, weed tops. You can even run your black and white junk mail through a shredder and add that. Don't compost bones.

diseased plants, household animal feces, oils and fats, seed heads, or weed roots.

Leaf mold is another great organic soil amendment that's easy to make. Pile up leaves from deciduous, hardwood trees in the fall. Keep the pile lightly moist, and turn it several times to speed up the process.

Your Plant Hardiness Zone

The term *hardiness* refers to a plant's ability to withstand cold temperatures. The hardiness rating is expressed as a numeric value called a zone, with some maps further divided into "a" or "b" sections, with the "a" sections being the colder

portion. The USDA Plant Hardiness Zone Map divides the United States, Canada, and Mexico into 11 color-coded zones which represent the lowest expected winter temperature in that area. Each zone is based on a 10-degree difference in minimum temperatures.

Once you know your hardiness zone, you'll have a valuable piece of information that you can use when choosing plants for your garden. Buy only plants that are hardy in your area—they'll survive the winters.

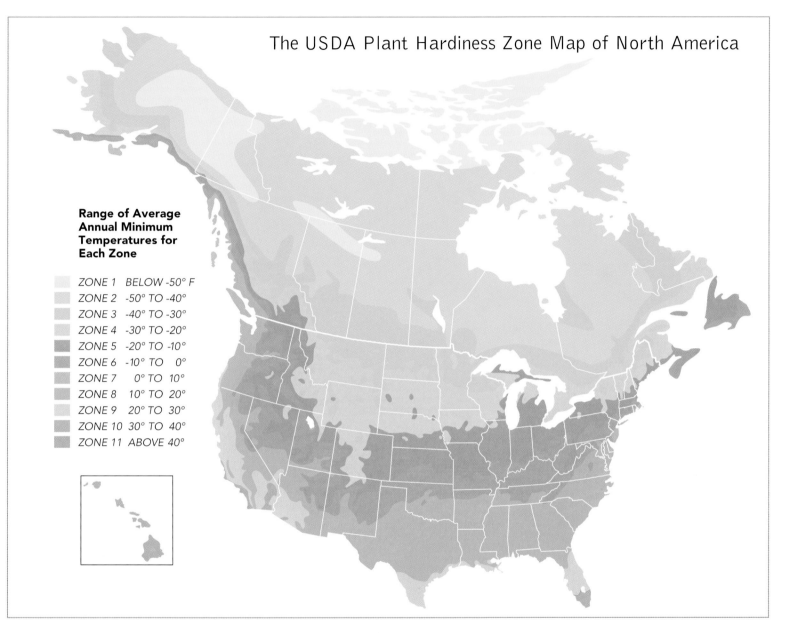

The USDA Plant Hardiness Zone Map of North America

Range of Average Annual Minimum Temperatures for Each Zone

ZONE 1   BELOW -50° F
ZONE 2   -50° TO -40°
ZONE 3   -40° TO -30°
ZONE 4   -30° TO -20°
ZONE 5   -20° TO -10°
ZONE 6   -10° TO   0°
ZONE 7   0° TO 10°
ZONE 8   10° TO 20°
ZONE 9   20° TO 30°
ZONE 10   30° TO 40°
ZONE 11 ABOVE 40°

Microclimates

not all areas in a garden are the same—one may be warmer or cooler— each is a different microclimate. For example, the wall of a building or a southern exposure creates a warmer microclimate, while a northern exposure makes a colder microclimate. So, a microclimate can function as a zone warmer or colder than the rest of the garden.

Once you're aware of microclimates, use them to your advantage. Extend the bloom season of a favorite plant up to a month by growing it in the cooler and warmer locations as well as in the normal part of the garden.

Gardeners like to push the envelope, growing plants with a warmer zone rating than their location allows. They can get away with this in a sheltered, south-facing spot. Conversely, certain plants might not survive in a windy spot, as it effectively has a lower zone rating.

Microclimates can be altered. Block prevailing winter winds by planting evergreens on the north side of the property. Plant deciduous trees on the south side to provide shade in summer.

Containers filled with plants enhance the area around them—whether they're used as accent plants on a deck or around a pool, container, it must have a drainage hole at the bottom. If a pot doesn't have a drainage hole, turn it into a miniature water garden.

A myriad of commercially-produced container shape and color. A single, large specimen can create drama—one large orange, banana, or bird- growing needs in the same container. Plants that prefer somewhat dry soil, moisture-loving plants, shade plants, and sun-lovers need separate containers.

When combining a number of plants in the containers retain moisture longer than clay pots. Clay pots absorb moisture, so they need extra watering.

Start with good soil. A good basic soil mix contains about one-third each of top soil, organic matter (peat moss, compost, or leaf mold), and perlite or sand. There is no need to cover the drainage holes in the bottom of the pot with pot shards or screening. In fact, they can keep the water from draining properly. Add a time-release fertilizer to give container plants a boost. Water as necessary, fertilize containers frequently, and they'll provide months of beauty anywhere in the garden.

gardening on a container scale

windowboxes attached to the house, or simple potted specimens plunged into an open spot in the border.

In a country garden, with its open and relaxed style, almost anything goes. "Found containers" add a whole new dimension to container gardening. An old watering can, log, wheelbarrow, boat, basket, work boot, or wooden box make striking planters.

Whatever the

pots—simple clay, plastic, and decorative pots—are readily available. Plastic weighs much less than clay and will withstand winter freezing. Manufacturers have improved the appearance of plastic containers, so many have a natural look.

Designing a Container Garden

the simplest container garden is a grouping of individual plants in similar containers. Create visual impact by massing a number of specimens while repeating the

of-paradise will attract attention. Group similar plants in a single container. A strawberry pot filled with herbs (near the kitchen door), an antique stone sink overflowing with different varieties of thyme, and a large basket of tropical houseplants are but a few possible choices. Remember to group plants with similar

same container, think of it as a miniature border—the same design principles apply. Vary the height (try stair-stepping the plants), mix textures, and control the color. Some theme containers might have a similar overall look with only subtle differences.

The major drawback to containers is that they dry out quickly on hot summer days. Plastic

The fun of container gardening is finding unusual pots and planters.

Fences

There are obvious, practical purposes for fences; they create privacy, block an undesirable view, and keep out intruders and animals. Fences also provide a backdrop for the garden, a canvas that shrubs and borders fill with promise and flowers. They can support wisteria, roses, clematis, and other vines

and climbers.

Historically, local materials were chosen for making fences because of availability and cost. Now, natural and man-made materials from all over the world are available from local suppliers. Fences are frequently constructed from the same material as the house. Whatever the material—wood, stone, or brick—fencing of the same material is consistent and tasteful. Although an exotic choice may be available, think carefully before choosing it. Local materials almost always blend naturally.

Country gardens suggest a relaxed approach to fencing. Today, most properties don't require a solid battlement as protection, although many gardeners do need protection from deer.

Open designs constructed of wood are frequent choices. White painted pickets with posts and finials of appropriate size and shape are classic. Weathered wood gives an even more casual look, as do pickets constructed of unpeeled saplings. Split rail fencing, constructed of rails split from logs and assembled without any nails, is a very simple

look which still defines a space but blocks very little sun or views. Woven wattle can work to protect your home and garden. Or use a lattice pattern to suggest woven wood.

Gates often are constructed of the same materials as the fencing, echoing or blending with the same style. Some gardeners have fun with their gates to express their personality—using a unique design pattern or color, or incorporating found materials, such as a piece of old metal fencing, or a wrought-iron headboard.

Arbors and Trellises

Arbors and trellises support climbing plants that would otherwise run along the ground or twine over and through shrubs and trees. These dramatic structures show off these plants in their best fashion.

Arbors and trellises also are decorative elements in a garden. Trellises can actually frame a garden or border. And, there is no greater joy than walking through an arbor dripping with wisteria or fragrant roses.

When building an arbor, don't skimp. Use sturdy materials. Painting or using a wood preservative will help it last years longer.

add **structures** for drama

Welcome Wildlife

gardens should be full of life: the wind rustling through ornamental grasses, scents tickling your nose, and most of all, birds singing, flying,

and splashing in the birdbath in your garden. There is a tremendous payoff for inviting birds into your landscape. They are enormously interesting to watch, especially in winter when there is less happening in the garden. Birds also provide natural pest control. Downy woodpeckers eat beetle larvae and moths;

black-capped chickadees devour caterpillars, flies, leafhoppers, and treehoppers; and white-breasted nuthatches dine on weevils, beetles, and ants. The sparkling-bright goldfinch consumes caterpillars along with some aphids.

Birds provide a level of joy that few other creatures can. With some effort, you can attract many species of birds and keep them

coming back to your own garden. If you provide food, water, and shelter, birds will be happily supplied with all that they need and will continue to make your garden their home.

Providing Natural Food for Birds

gardeners can plant a beautiful garden that's also a feast for feathered friends. You improve your local environment when you grow a food supply for the birds.

Berries, nuts, seeds,

and nectar are types of food needed by different species of birds. Select a combination of plants that will provide food throughout the year, especially those that bear fruit or seed from

late winter until the next winter. Supplement the birds' diet with a steady supply of seed, suet, or fruit (depending on the species you want to

attract). Allow some annuals and perennial plants to go to seed; the seeds can supply food for cardinals and finches. Also, add some plants that retain berries through the winter.

Bird Feeders

You can supplement the natural food by adding bird feeders to your garden and providing

seed for your winged friends. There really are no "squirrelproof" feeders, so use baffles to deter them. Some gardeners feed whole ears of corn to the squirrels to keep them away from the bird feeders. Place your feeders in open locations so that cats and other predators find it hard to ambush feeding birds. Be consistent; keep your feeder filled with appropriate and nutritious food. Learn about the preferred food of the birds you wish to attract by consulting a field guide to birds and by observing the birds in your area.

attracting birds to the garden

Water Sources

Cardinals, finches, grackles, jays, juncos, mockingbirds, and sparrows flock to feeders on the ground, while chickadees, finches, sparrows, titmice, warblers, and woodpeckers seek out hanging feeders. Use a

post to create a platform for your feeder. Flat feeders lure chickadees, finches, flickers, jays, mockingbirds, nuthatches, and wrens. In winter, put suet in a mesh bag and hang it from a tree to draw chickadees, flickers, mockingbirds, and woodpeckers.

a simple birdbath makes a nice decorative element in the country garden and provides needed water for the birds. Keep water from freezing in winter by using a small heater sold for that purpose. Clean your water source often. Birds remember where water is located and will return to your garden every day for a drink or a refreshing bath. Many birds frolic in the water and offer hours of enjoyment. Robins splash in birdbaths, and warblers swoop and play in the spray of water from sprinklers or fountains.

A naturalistic garden is perfect for a small pond or pool—one with a modest waterfall and rock edging. Frogs and toads, great gobblers of mosquitoes and other winged pests as well as

other wildlife, are drawn to the water. But even if you don't have a stream or can't build a pond, you can create a constant source of water. Any shallow container (2 to 3 inches deep) is sufficient. Clay saucers and inverted trashcan lids can do the trick, but adding extra birdbaths is more attractive.

Safe Haven

b irds need safe spots to build their nests, mate, rest, hide from predators, raise their young, and fine shelter from the cold, wind, and rain. Evergreen trees and broad-leaf evergreen shrubs are particularly appealing to them in winter. Birds seek a variety of locations for their homes. Some prefer low, near-the-

ground spots. A thicket of shrubs or brambles is perfect for some birds. Others are lured to foundation plantings.

Leave an unmown strip at the edge of your property or plant a small meadow. Islands of shrubs and trees are habitats for a variety of

birds. Underplant tall trees with shrubs and groundcovers to create nesting areas. Even a dead tree can be a home, hiding place, or food supply for some birds. If you can't leave dead trees on your property, add a few logs to a shrub border. Also, birdhouses make fun additions to the garden, giving homes to the birds you wish to attract.

Birds make a garden come alive with movement and music. Feeding them year-round ensures their constant company.

Plant bird-attracting flowers such as purple coneflowers. Birds will pick on seed heads all winter.

Attracting Hummingbirds

hummingbirds cause unusual excitement for everyone. They are so small and flit so fast, sometimes you're not certain you've actually seen one at all. Then they return to feed, and you have another chance to observe them. They zip over the deck and fly by a young child who exclaims with joy at seeing flashes of color in the sunlight. "Hummers," as they're called, can hover, fly backwards, and reach speeds of 60 miles per hour in seconds. Their wings move so fast that they seem to blur on each side of their diminutive bodies. That wing movement creates the low hum you hear when they are in flight. Once you've experienced this, you'll want to bring the magic of hummingbirds into your gardens and your life.

Ten species of hummingbirds migrate north of the Mexican border each summer. Only the ruby-throated hummingbird is seen east of the Mississippi River. The ruby-throat makes the 500-mile trip across the Gulf of Mexico in one nonstop flight. It's a tiny creature, only 3 inches long, weighing only 3 grams—$\frac{1}{10}$ of an ounce. Yet, it's fearless, attacking crows and eagles that venture into its territory. The ruby-throat lays tiny eggs, each one smaller than a jellybean.

Basics for a Hummingbird Garden

hummingbirds need food, water, and shelter just as other birds, but adapted to their needs. Hummers prefer red tubular flowers; these offer sources of nectar.

Dense plantings provide safe nesting spots. Hummingbirds also need open areas for sunlight and warmth, and room to fly.

Avoid the use of pesticides around any birds; hummingbirds' small size makes them particularly susceptible to harm. They consume many small insects, along with flower nectar, which puts them at greater risk for environmental contamination.

Flowers for Hummingbirds

red is hummingbirds' first choice in flowers, although they'll visit plants of other colors and dine at those nectar sources. They will even investigate red-patterned clothes.

Hummingbirds also seek out flowers with a long tubular shape, which are specifically adapted to be used by the hummingbird's long, needle-sized tongue to extract nectar unreachable by bees and butterflies. In exchange for the nectar, the hummingbirds are very effective pollinators of their food sources. When pushing their heads into the flowers, they brush their heads or bills against the sticky pollen, which is then carried to, and pollinates, the next flower.

Hummers visit hundreds of flowers

each day, so grow a variety of flowers for them. Garden annuals, such as red salvias and fuchsias, bloom all season and provide food throughout the summer. Plant them generously in beds and borders, and at the edge of an open, sunny lawn.

Add several different houses to attract a variety of bird species.

Hummingbird Feeders

Hanging baskets, windowboxes, and container plantings for decks and living areas bring hummers right to you. Because of their fearless ways, they will make frequent eating trips to food sources that are positioned only a few feet from where you may be sitting.

Supplemental feeders also satisfy hummingbirds' voracious appetites. Select ones with bee and ant deterrents built in, or add them to your feeders. Hang feeders in shady locations, under a tree, on a porch or deck. If you use multiple feeders, separate them by at least 6 feet and keep them out of sight of one another. Hummers are very territorial—careful placement prevents squabbles.

Fill feeders with a solution of refined white sugar and water (one part to four parts). Boil this solution to dissolve the sugar, kill bacteria, prevent mold, and slow fermentation. Don't leave the solution in the feeder longer than two days. Clean the feeder well every few days.

Commercially-made feeders have red on them so there is no need—and it may be dangerous to the hummers—to add red food color to the sugar-water solution. Never use honey or artificial sweeteners. Honey ferments easily, can be fatal to the birds, and the sweeteners have no nutritive value. Ready-made mixtures also are available.

Natural Foods for Songbirds and Hummingbirds

trees

- Birch (*Betula* spp.)
- Cherry (*Prunus* spp.)
- Crabapple (*Malus* spp.)
- Dogwood (*Cornus* spp.)
- Eastern red cedar (*Juniperus virginiana*)
- Hawthorn (*Crataegus* spp.)
- Serviceberry (*Amelanchier* spp.)
- Silk tree (*Albizia julibrissin*)*
- Spruce (*Picea* spp.)

shrubs

- Bayberry (*Myrica pensylvanica*)
- Beautybush (*Kolkwitzia* spp.)*
- Chaste tree (*Vitex agnus-castus*)*
- Cotoneaster (*Cotoneaster* spp.)
- Elderberry (*Sambucus canadensis*)
- Hardy fuchsia (*Fuchsia magellanica*)*
- Holly (*Ilex verticillata* and others)
- Juniper (*Juniperus* spp.)
- Spicebush (*Lindera benzoin*)
- Sumac (*Rhus* spp.)
- Viburnum (*Viburnum* spp.)
- Weigela (*Weigela florida*)*

vines

- Boston ivy/Virginia creeper (*Parthenocissus* spp.)
- Firethorn (*Pyracantha* spp.)
- Grapes (*Vitis* spp.)
- Honeysuckle (*Lonicera* spp.)*
- Morning glory (*Ipomoea* spp.)
- Scarlet runner bean (*Phaseolus coccineus*)*
- Trumpet vine (*Campsis radicans*)*

perennials

- Asters (*Aster* spp.)
- Beard-tongue (*Penstemon* spp.)*
- Bee balm (*Monarda didyma*)*
- Black-eyed Susan (*Rudbeckia* spp.)
- Butterfly weed (*Asclepias tuberosa*)*
- Columbine (*Aquilegia* spp.)*
- Coneflower (*Echinacea* spp.)
- Coral bells (*Heuchera* spp.)*
- Foxglove (*Digitalis* spp.)*
- Goldenrod (*Solidago* spp.)

annuals

- Bachelor's button (*Centaurea cyanus*)
- Cosmos (*Cosmos* spp.)
- Fuchsia (*Fuchsia* x *hybrida*)*
- Marigold (*Tagetes* spp.)
- Pineapple sage (*Salvia elegans*)*
- Red salvia (*Salvia splendens*)*
- Zinnia (*Zinnia elegans*)

*Indicates plants that also supply food for hummingbirds.

Butterflies find nectarous flowers such as zinnias and butterfly bush.

The Beauty of Butterflies

The graceful movement, alluring beauty, and color of butterflies attract humans. Part of it is also the fascination with their metamorphoses and their flight endurance—watching them through their life stages.

Like hummingbirds, butterflies need nectar-laden flowers to survive. They prefer spikes of numerous, tiny flowers (clustered flowers) or flat heads of daisylike flowers where they can land or perch. They also favor fragrant flowers. Along with a food source, butterflies need shelter, sun, and water.

Butterfly Plants

The large mass of a single flower attracts more butterflies than individual flowers

scattered throughout a border. Butterflies don't see color as humans do so they aren't drawn to the most colorful or brightest plants. Instead, ultraviolet color patterns and scent lure them to particular plants.

Site your butterfly garden in full sun away from prevailing winds. A living barrier, like a hedge, or a manmade structure, such as fencing, is protection from adverse weather conditions.

bringing butterflies home

Food for Caterpillars

Part of the appeal of butterflies is the miracle of their transformation. This metamorphosis takes them from the egg stage, to the caterpillar, the pupa, or chrysalis, and finally, the gorgeous

adult butterfly stage. Gardeners also must supply food sources for the caterpillar stage (or at least be willing to share some of the garden's bounty with them). The caterpillar lives and eats for several weeks, getting bigger

and bigger, eating its way through foliage and flowers of its preferred host plant. Most of the butterflies we love and wish to attract are first caterpillars that feed on weeds or on trees and

shrubs, which can withstand the destructive grazing. Black swallowtail caterpillars are quite fond of plants in the carrot family: parsley, fennel, dill, carrots, and the weed, Queen Anne's lace. Monarch caterpillars feed only on the milkweed family.

Water for Butterflies

Mud puddles are a favorite source of water for butterflies. To supplement this natural source, gardeners need to create a similar and shallow supply for them. Use a shallow container filled with sand and water and sunk into the ground in a sunny spot.

Nectarous plants, such as this Mexican sunflower, are butterfly magnets.

Butterfly hibernation boxes give non-migrating species a place to spend the winter.

For a different look, use large seashells such as scallop or clam.

Butterflies are cold-blooded, so include some flat rocks where they can sun themselves and warm up their wings enough to fly.

Housing for Butterflies

Many species of butterflies migrate to warmer climates in winter. For example, monarchs fly to Southern California and Mexico for their winter migration. However, there are species that overwinter, even in areas that require cold weather. Butterfly hibernation boxes may provide butterflies with a spot to stay for the winter. Generally, these butterflies that do hibernate look for wood piles and brush in wooded areas. Hibernating butterflies include commas, tortoiseshells, and mourning cloaks.

Moths, Too

Moths, generally nocturnal, are equally fascinating. Unfortunately, they're often maligned as a group because of pest species. Grow some night-blooming plants, such as flowering tobacco and angel's trumpet, and you'll discover the splendor of luna and sphinx moths as they flit in the moonlight garden.

Natural Foods for Butterflies

trees

- Black locust (*Robinia pseudoacacia*)*
- Dogwood (*Cornus* spp.)*
- Tulip tree (*Liriodendron tulipifera*)*

shrubs

- Azaleas (*Rhododendron* spp.)
- Butterfly bush (*Buddleia davidii*)
- Glossy abelia (*Abelia* x *grandiflora*)
- Lilac (*Rhododendron* spp.)
- Pussy willow (*Salix caprea*)
- Rhododendrons (*Rhododendron* spp.)
- Spicebush (*Lindera benzoin*)*

annuals and herbs

- Blanket flower (*Gaillardia pulchella*)
- Blue daisy (*Felicia amelloides*)
- Butterfly plant (*Schizanthus pinnatus*)
- China pinks (*Dianthus chinensis*)
- Cosmos (*Cosmos* spp.)
- Creeping zinnia (*Sanvitalia procumbens*)
- Dill (*Anethum graveolens*)*
- Fennel (*Foeniculum vulgare*)*
- Flossflower (*Ageratum houstonianum*)
- Golden coreopsis (*Coreopsis tinctoria*)
- Heliotrope (*Heliotropium arborescens*)
- Larkspur (*Consolida ambigua*)
- Parsley (*Petroselinum crispum*)*
- Petunia (*Petunia* x *hybrida*)
- Phlox (*Phlox drummondii*)
- Snapdragon (*Antirrhinum majus*)*
- Strawflower (*Helichrysum bracteatum*)
- Zinnia (*Zinnia elegans*)

perennials and biennials

- Aster (*Aster* spp.)
- Black-eyed Susan (*Rudbeckia* spp.)
- Borage (*Borago officinalis*)*
- Butterfly weed (*Asclepias tuberosa*)*
- Candytuft (*Iberis sempervirens*)
- Goldenrod (*Solidago* spp.)
- Hollyhock (*Alcea rosea*)*
- Japanese anemone (*Anemone* x *hybrida*)
- Joe-Pye weed (*Eupatorium purpureum*)
- Lavender (*Lavendula* spp.)
- Purple coneflower (*Echinacea purpurea*)
- Sunflower (*Helianthus* spp.)
- Coreopsis (*Coreopsis* spp.)
- Wild blue indigo (*Baptisia australis*)
- Yarrow (*Achillea* spp.)

*Indicates plants that also supply food for caterpillars.

mail-order plant sources

a Appalachian Gardens (P-free)
Box 82
Waynesboro, PA 17268-0082
717-762-4312

b W. Atlee Burpee & Co. (S-free)
300 Park Avenue
Warminster, PA 18974-0001
800-333-5808

c Busse Gardens (P-$2)
5873 Oliver Avenue S.W.
Cokato, MN 55321-4229
320-286-2654

d Daffodil Mart (B-$1)
30 Irene Street
Torrington, CT 06790
800-255-2852

e Forestfarm (P-$4)
990 Tetherow Rd.
Williams, OR 97544-9599
541-846-7269

f Goodwin Creek Gardens (P-$2)
PO Box 83
Williams, OR 97544

g Greer Gardens (P-$3)
1280 Goodpasture Island Rd.
Eugene, OR 97401-1794
541-686-8266

h Gossler Farms Nursery (P-$4)
1200 Weaver Rd.
Springfield, OR 97478-9691
541-746-3922

i Heronswood Nursery Ltd. (P-$5)
7530 NE 288th
Kingston, WA 98346-9502
360-297-4172

j J.L. Hudson, Seedsman (S-$1)
Star Route 2, Box 337
La Honda, CA 94020
No telephone

k Johnny's Selected Seed (S-free)
Foss Hill Rd.
Albion, ME 04910-9731
207-437-4301

l Klehm Nursery (P-$5)
4210 North Duncan Rd.
Champaign, IL 61821
800-553-3715

m Lilypons Water Gardens
(P-$5)
PO Box 10
Buckeystown, MD 21717-0010
800-999-5459

n Louisiana Nursery (P-$5)
5853 Highway 182
Opelousas, LA 70570
318-948-3696

o Logee's Greenhouses (P-$3)
141 North St.
Danielson, CT 06239
800-774-8038

p J. E. Miller Nurseries (P-free)
5060 West Lake Rd.
Canandaigua, NY 14424
800-836-9630

q Niche Gardens (P-$3)
1111 Dawson Road
Chapel Hill, NC 27516
919-967-0078

r Nichols Garden Nursery (S-free)
1190 Old Salem Road NE
Albany, OR 97321-4542
541-928-9280

s Park Seed (S-free)
1 Parkton Avenue
Greenwood, SC 29647-0001
864-223-7333

t Pinetree Garden Seed (S-free)
Box 300
New Gloucester, ME 04260
207-926-3400

u Plant Delights Nursery (P-$2)
9241 Sauls Road
Raleigh, NC 27603
919-772-4794

v Richters (P, S-$2)
357 Highway 47
Goodwood
Ontario L0C 1A0 Canada
905-640-6677

w Rock Spray Nursery (P-free)
Box 693
Truro, MA 02666-0693
508-349-6769

x Roses of Yesterday & Today
(Arena Rose Company) (P-$3)
PO Box 3096
Paso Robles, CA 93477
805-227-4094

y Roslyn Nursery (P-$2)
211 Burrs Lane
Dix Hills, NY 11746
516-643-9347

z Select Seeds (S-$3)
180 Stickney Hill Rd.
Stafford Springs, CT 06076-4617
860-684-9310

aa Shady Oaks Nursery (P-$2)
112 10th Avenue S.E.
Waseca, MN 56093
507-835-5033

bb Siskiyou Rare Plant Nursery
(P-$3)
2825 Cummings Rd.
Medford, OR 97501-1538
541-746-3922

cc Stokes Seed (S-free)
Box 548
Buffalo, NY 11746
716-695-6980

dd Thompson & Morgan (S-free)
PO Box 1308
Jackson, NJ 08527-0308
800-274-7333

ee Tranquil Lake Nursery (P-$1)
45 River Street
Rehoboth, MA 02769-1395
508-252-4002

ff Twombly Nursery (P-$4)
163 Barn Hill Rd.
Monroe, CT 06468
203-261-2133

gg Wayside Gardens (P-free)
1 Garden Lane
Hodges, SC 29695-0001
800-845-1124

hh We-Du Nurseries (P-$2)
Route 5, Box 724
Marion, NC 28752-9338
704-738-8300

ii White Flower Farm (P-free)
PO Box 50
Litchfield, CT 06759-0050
800-503-9624

jj Woodlanders (P-$2)
1128 Colleton Avenue
Aiken, SC 29801
803-648-7522

(P) Plants	(B) Bulbs
(S) Seed	($0) Price of catalog

plant index

Page references in *italics* indicate photographs.

a

Abelia
glossy, 10, 11
x *grandiflora*, 11
Acer
palmatum 'Sango Kaku', *94*
platanoides, 45
pseudoplatanus, 102
Achillea
'Apple Blossom', *61*
'Coronation Gold', *12, 76*
filipendulina, 86
millefolium
'Paprika', *169*
'Summer Pastels', *142*
'Moonshine', *35*
Aconitum napellus, 160
Adiantum pedatum, 52, 141
Ageratum, 26, 85
hardy, 56
houstonianum
'Blue Danube', *86*
Alberta spruce, dwarf, *138,* 139
Alcea rosea
'Outhouse Hollyhocks', *44*
Alchemilla mollis, 125, 169
Alkanet, 112, 124
Allium, 26
schoenoprasum, 70, 106, 171
Aloysia triphylla, 50
Althea zebrina, 143
Alstroemeria, 133
Alyssum, sweet, *42, 128, 130, 158, 162*
Amaranth, globe, 28, *29*
Amelanchier canadensis, 102
Amsonia tabernaemontana, 113
Anchusa azurea, 112, 124
Anemone, 93
x *hybrida*, 76
Japanese, 56, 76, 90
tomentosa, 96
Apple mint, 50, *52*

Aquilegia
alpina, 124, *163*
caerulea
'Crimson Star', *77*
canadensis, *169*
'Nora Barlow', *13*
Arborvitae, 120, *121*
Argyranthemum frutescens, 44
Artemisia, 93
abrotanum 'Lemon Scented', *69*
annua, 26
dracunculus, 68
'Silver King', 26
'Silver Mound', *26,* 90, 96
Asclepias tuberosa, 16
Asiatic lily, 32, 42, *44,* 112, *115, 158, 160*
Aster, 139
New England, 139, *142*
novae-angliae, 142
tataricus, 145
Astilbe, 8, 10, 12, 34, 42, 56, 74, 76, 93, 136, 139
x *arendsii*, 34, *138*
'Weisse Gloria', *92*
chinensis
'Fanal', *78*
'Veronica Klose', *44*
Aucuba, 18
japonica, 22
Azalea, 32
G. G. Gurbling, 82
Kurume, 34, *36*
swamp, 18, *19*

b

Baby's breath, 26, *28*
Bachelor's-button, 26
Balloon flower, 139, *140*
Balsam, garden, 112, *115*
Bamboo, heavenly, 10, *13,* 120, *124*
Baptisia australis, 97
Barberry, 158, *159*

Basil
lettuce-leaf, 168, *169*
purple, 150, *151*
Beach rose, 102
Bearded iris, 10, *12,* 76, *79,* 93, *94,* 158, *160*
Beard-tongue, 34, *37,* 120, *122, 130,* 131
Beautyberry, 16, 18, *20*
Beautybush, 158, *160*
Bee balm, *38,* 42, *44,* 66, 69, 82
Bellflower, 120, 124, 139, 141, 163
clustered, 158,
peach-leafed, 10, *12,* 76, 79
Bellis perennis, 60, *170*
Bells-of-Ireland, 28, *29*
Berberis thunbergii 'Aurea', *159*
Berries, 16
Betula nigra 'Heritage', *36*
Big blue lilyturf, 18, *19*
Birch, river, 34, *36*
Bird's nest spruce, *138,* 139
Black-eyed Susan, 10, *11,* 18, *19, 54, 58, 84,* 85
Blanket flower, 10, *11*
Bleeding heart, 58, *59,* 136, 139, *143*
Bloodroot, 56
Blue Douglas fir, 34, *36*
Blue false indigo, 93, 97
Blue oat grass, *92,* 93
Bluebeard, 76, 120, *125*
Blue spruce, 42
Bluestar, 112, *113*
Boxwood, 48
Dwarf, 110
Korean, 18, *19,* 150, *151*
Buddleia davidii, 22
'Nanho Blue', *35*
Bugloss, *112,* 120, *124*
Bulbs, 48, 128, 156. See also *specific species*
Butterfly bush, 18, *22,* 32, 34, *35*
Butterfly iris, 34, *35*
Butterfly weed, 16
Buxus microphylla var. *koreana, 19, 151*

C

Calendula, 66, 100, 105, 126, 128, 131
officinalis, 70, *104, 133*
California poppy, 46, 50, *51*
Calla lily, 60, 93, *98*
Callicarpa japonica, 20
Calluna vulgaris 'Lyndon Proudly', *10*
Camellia, 82, 93
sasanqua, 94
Campanula
glomerata, *163*
latifolia, 124
persicifolia, *12,* 79
portenschlagiana, *141*
Campsis radicans, 67, *151*
Canterbury bells, 110
Cape fuschsia, 120, *123*
Cardinal flower, 10, *11*
Carolina jasmine, 48
Caryopteris x *clandonensis*
'Blue Mist', 76, *125*
Catmint, 120, *124*
Cattail, 150, *151*
Celandine poppy, 74
Celosia, 26
argentea var. *cristata*
'Sparkler Hybrids', *28*
Centaurea montana, *125*
Centranthus ruber, 85, *96*
Cerastium tomentosum, *142*
Cercis chinensis, *43*
Chamaemelum nobile, 10
Chamomile, 8, *10*
Cherry, weeping, 32
Chinese redbud, 42, *43*
Chives, 66, 70, *105,* 106, 168, *171*
Christmas fern, 136
Christmas rose, 56
Chrysanthemum, 18, 21, 42, 43, 139, 140
frutescens, 44
leucanthemum, *19, 51, 99,* 112, *162*
nipponicum, 113
x *moriflorium*, *21,* 140
x *superbum*, *43,* 106
Cicely, sweet, 66, 70

Acknowledgements

We wish to thank the following people, whose gardens originally appeared in the pages of Country Home® *Country Gardens*:
Kristin and Craig Beddow
Steve Carruthers
Dolores Cakebread
Lynn and Maurice de la Valetta
Michael and Kate Eagleton
Eric E. Fitzpatrick
Pamela Gladding
Tom Hinz
David and Carolyn Pettengill Jenson
Ed and Carol King
June Kroft
Helaine Mackey
Katherine Macy
Harold and Julia Pierce
Betty and Reimert Ravenholt
Mary Reedy
Frederick Rice
Jeanne Rose
Ann and Joe Snuggs

And thanks to C. Colston Burrell for the use of his garden for cover photography.

metric conversions

U.S. Units to Metric Equivalent			Metric Units to U.S. Equivalents		
To Convert From	*Multiply By*	*To Get*	*To Convert From*	*Multiply By*	*To Get*
Inches	25.4	Millimetres	Millimetres	0.0394	Inches
Inches	2.54	Centimetres	Centimetres	0.3937	Inches
Feet	30.48	Centimetres	Centimetres	0.0328	Feet
Feet	0.3048	Metres	Metres	3.2808	Feet
Yards	0.9144	Metres	Metres	1.0936	Yards
Square inches	6.4516	Square centimetres	Square centimetres	0.1550	Square inches
Square feet	0.0929	Square metres	Square metres	10.764	Square feet
Square yards	0.8361	Square metres	Square metres	1.1960	Square yards
Acres	0.4047	Hectares	Hectares	2.4711	Acres
Cubic inches	16.387	Cubic centimetres	Cubic centimetres	0.0610	Cubic inches
Cubic feet	0.0283	Cubic metres	Cubic metres	35.315	Cubic feet
Cubic feet	28.316	Litres	Litres	0.0353	Cubic feet
Cubic yards	0.7646	Cubic metres	Cubic metres	1.308	Cubic yards
Cubic yards	764.55	Litres	Litres	0.0013	Cubic yards

To convert from degrees Fahrenheit (F) to degrees Celsius (C), first subtract 32, then multiply by 5/9.

To convert from degrees Celsius to degrees Fahrenheit, multiply by 9/5, then add 32.